The
Slim
Solution

Karl Henry is one Ireland's leading personal trainers, well known for his work on TV's *Operation Transformation* and responsible for creating some of the most famous physiques in fashion, music, politics and industry.

He holds a BSc (hons) Sports Management from University College Dublin along with personal training qualifications, and is currently studying for an exercise and nutrition masters science degree.

Karl has a weekly health column in the *Irish Independent*, and is regular contributor to TV and radio on health matters.

As well as his personal training and media work, he regularly lectures on fitness and wellbeing, and is a self-described fitness fanatic, each year finding a new sport to further his knowledge to pass on to his clients. His interests include hill-walking, cycling, triathlon, swimming, mountain biking, kite surfing, surfing, marathons, ironman triathlons and, more recently, ultra-marathons.

The Slim Solution

KARL HENRY

HACHETTE
BOOKS
IRELAND

First published in 2013 by Hachette Books Ireland
A division of Hachette UK Ltd.

A CIP catalogue record for this title is available from the British Library.

ISBN 978 1444 744040

Typeset and layout design by redrattledesign.com
Cover design by www.anu-design.ie
Author cover and inside photos by Partick Bolger

Printed and bound by Clays Ltd, St Ives plc

Hachette Books Ireland policy is to use papers that are natural, renewable and recyclable products and made from wood grown in sustainable forests. The logging and manufacturing processes are expected to conform to the environmental regulations of the country of origin.

Hachette Books Ireland
8 Castlecourt Centre
Castleknock
Dublin 15, Ireland

A division of Hachette UK Ltd
338 Euston Road
London NW1 3BH
www.hachette.ie

This book is dedicated to you, the reader, who has taken the first step to changing your life. The content within these pages will give you the tools to do just that, but you have done the hard part and taken the first step. Now it's time to realise your potential and achieve your best.

As Roy Rogers always said, Happy trails . . .

CONTENTS

MY MESSAGE

I am lucky: I get to promote the virtues of healthy living and exercise to large groups of people through newspapers, television and radio. Unlike so many other authors, I am not trying to promote an unhealthy quick-fix solution that will only work in the short term, nor am I trying to sell you any branded products. I believe that you *can* be healthy for life: you *can* be healthier, fitter and slimmer all year round. You *can* become more motivated, more focused and more successful by following the 30-day method that I have created in the Slim Solution. By eating healthily and moving more in the right way, kick-starting the body to get healthy, there is no reason that you can't. I will personally guide you through the 30 days to help you create healthy habits.

My message is about balance:

- Have your treat day once a week.

- Don't try to give up your favourite foods altogether.

- Don't try to exercise every day.

- Don't try to cut out certain food groups.

I am not the stereotypical ego-fuelled personal trainer:

- My weight goes up and down, just like yours.

- I know what it is to be overweight – I'm living proof that my method works.

- I have been unhealthy and struggled to motivate myself when my energy levels were low.

- I have been there and I know how you feel, how you are thinking and also how to break those habits .

This is what the Slim Solution is all about.

I have seen literally hundreds of clients achieve their goals using the tools that I will be giving you. You will be following a specific day-by-day guide that will take you through the 30 days. I will be teaching you how to break those sugar cravings, reintroduce exercise into your life and eat the way our bodies are designed to. I will be giving you rest days and treat days and keeping you motivated. Are you excited? Are you ready to make those changes? Are you ready to start the Slim Solution?

PHASE ONE

INTRODUCTION

Do you want to

- Improve your life for the better?

- Change the shape of your body?

- Lose weight?

- Reduce your medical bills?

- Improve your fitness levels?

- Stop getting out of breath when you walk?

- Sleep better?

- Live longer and healthier?

- Have more energy?

- Fit into your clothes better?

If the answer to any of the above questions is yes, then I believe this is the book for you. I know, you have seen promises to tackle these issues in many other books, year after year – so what makes this book different? The reality is that I won't try to trick you with gimmicks or methods that don't work in real life. Through hard work and my guidance, you will be amazed at what you can achieve. And best of all, if you follow the method in the Slim Solution you can achieve the above in just 30 days.

This is a tried-and-tested plan I have created through years of experience with my clients. I have seen what an incredible difference it can make in such a short time, and by setting some simple targets at the very beginning and working towards them with me, the method will change your life.

I will teach you how to eat healthily – through the 30 days and beyond. You will have all the information you need to lose weight without eliminating any food groups or resorting to quick fixes, as with so many other diets on the market. You'll see first-hand that carbohydrates aren't the problem in terms of gaining weight. Real weight loss is about balance and moderation, combined with hard work.

I will then outline your exercise plan, using all of my knowledge and skills to keep you motivated through every pitfall that has stopped you from succeeding before.

By following me through the 30 days of the Slim Solution, you will learn things about yourself you never knew, helping you to reach for the stars and achieve things you never thought possible. Sustainability is a cornerstone of the Slim Solution. It is about changing and improving your life in the long term. I want to get you fit for life, not give you a quick fix where you push yourself to breaking point and end up putting all the weight you've lost back on.

BUT I AM TOO BUSY

Like my clients, you are a busy person with many commitments. You need a plan that can fit into your life without taking it over. In this book I introduce an exercise regime that won't leave you in pain for days on end and a food plan that will satisfy you, not leave you craving your favourite foods.

I will show you just how easy losing weight and getting fit can be (yes, it is easy); I will show you what a difference being healthy can make to how you feel, think and interact with those around you, leaving you with only one question: why haven't I done it before?

By seeing how good you can feel by changing your diet and exercising more, you will think differently about exercise. Once you see the benefits, you will become self-motivated so that all you have learned becomes second nature.

I have been lucky enough to have written two bestselling health books, and the Slim Solution features new exercises and a whole new method to make losing weight even easier. It's about something more than weight loss – it is about how you think and feel about your life and what you can achieve in it. So why not let me become your personal trainer and help you become the healthiest, fittest and happiest you have ever been?

1

WHAT CAN YOU ACHIEVE?

FEEL

TRUST

KNOW

You will be amazed at what you can achieve in just 30 days. I have seen clients drop a dress size, reduce their cholesterol and blood pressure and improve lower-back problems simply by eating healthier and moving more. They have become more focused and driven, more motivated and less stressed. They followed exactly what I am going to outline for you in this book, doing the same exercises and eating the same foods.

Are you willing to commit just four weeks to making changes that will last the rest of your life? If so then these are the types of results you can expect:

- **8–21 pounds of weight loss:** Depending on how much weight you have to lose and how unhealthy you are, you will be able to lose different amounts of weight.

Remember that in the first week you will be losing fluid and toxins that have built up in your system over the years, so you will obtain a bigger result than in subsequent weeks – this can act as a great motivator but don't focus too much on it.

- **Up to six inches off your waist:** Waistlines expand because of the foods that we eat and drink. The modern diet is full of starch and yeast and other ingredients that ferment in the gut, leaving you feeling overly full and bloated. Combine this with lack of movement and it is no wonder that your jeans are tighter and your belt has to be loosened another notch. In the 30 days you will be eliminating, for the most part, all the refined and processed foods that are causing the problem, leading to a flatter and firmer stomach and helping you to be more confident in your clothes and in yourself.

- **No longer getting out of breath:** In my Slim Solution plan, I will be showing you how to walk properly, ensuring that you are getting the most out of your sessions and pushing your lungs so that you get fitter. Whether it is running for the bus, walking up a flight of stairs or simply chasing after your children, you will feel confident and amazed at the difference such a short time can make to your fitness levels.

- **Leaner and more toned:** Muscle is not the same as fat – they are totally different and can't turn into each other. As you progress through the 30 days, you will notice your body fat decreasing and your muscle tone increasing. I will be giving you specific exercises to get your body looking firm, without looking bulky or athletic. You will have less wobble when you look in the mirror and will have a new-found confidence when dressed, being proud to show off that body you have worked so hard for.

- **Dropping a dress size:** For most women, one stone is the equivalent to a dress size and I have seen so many people drop a dress size in 30 days by following this exact plan – not only that but they continue to lose weight, growing healthier and fitter after the 30 days are up. Once you get used to feeling healthy and realise just how easy it can be, you will never want to go back.

- **Feeling more focused and motivated:** From working through the 30 days, you will naturally become more driven, focused and motivated than ever before. Making these changes to your diet and lifestyle will affect everything about you and how you think. It is hard to get motivated when you have poor energy levels and feel that life is just one big stress cycle – once you break this cycle, you will be able to make the changes you wanted and I will be there to help you along the way.

- **A healthy, happier new you:** The healthier you are, the happier you will be. Health affects everything you do, every relationship you have, both in work and at home, and pretty much all of your life.

By eating healthier and exercising, you will become energised, motivated and generally happier in your own skin. This happiness will radiate and improve your relationships with those around you.

COMMON GOALS

We all know that men and women are different and think differently. Well, when it comes to health and weight loss, guess what? Their goals are different too! The next crucial part of any journey for health is setting the right goals. In this section I will bring you some background on specific goals that my male and female clients have had and how realistic they are to achieve.

WHAT DO WOMEN WANT?

The question that all men would like to know the answer to! But when it comes to weight loss and getting fit, there are some common goals that I see regularly.

- *A flatter tummy:* Who doesn't want one of these?! Your stomach is one area of

23

the body that affects all of your clothes and how you look and feel in them. It is an incredibly sensitive area and can bloat instantly because of certain foods and drinks. Over the 30-day plan you can flatten your stomach dramatically. Actually, you can do this in seven days if you want. And the good news is that you don't have to do lots of sit-ups to achieve it (sit-ups actually have very little effect on your stomach). Food is the critical change here and the 30-day Slim Solution will show you just how critical!

- *Firmer legs:* The legs are a big muscle group in the body and there are simple exercises that can actually make them look longer as well as giving them more shape. Firming up the legs will take hard work and a change in your foods but you will see a difference very quickly. The firmer and stronger the legs are, the less pressure that is placed upon the joints, so you are benefiting in every way!

- *More shapely arms:* One of the areas where women store fat is on the arms, specifically the backs of the arms, also known as bingo wings – the soft tissue here can cause women a lot of grief. As you grow older, the shape of your arms will begin to change and, while I can't give you the arms you had in your twenties, I can help you to tone them up and give them back some shape.

- *Less cellulite:* Cellulite, the bane of so many women and sometimes even men. Cellulite forms when your body runs out of space where it forms toxins and fat. These have nowhere else to go and eventually push through the skin, creating the lumpy effect that bothers so many people. To reduce your cellulite you need to move more and eat a cleaner diet, just like the one in this plan. Massage is also fantastic for cellulite but it needs to be a deep massage, which can often be painful. Plenty of water is also a good idea, as it will help to flush out the toxins!

- *More energy:* One of the problems with being unhealthy, unfit and overweight is lack of energy. You feel lethargic all of the time. If this sounds familiar to you, then wait until you see the difference 30 days can make! By reducing the amount of processed food in your diet and exercising more, you will dramatically increase the amount of energy you have. You will sleep better and deeper too.

- *Improve PMS symptoms:* Exercise and healthy eating are two of the easiest ways to improve the effects of your period. From bloating to fluid retention to mood swings, the method will make a significant difference to all of these.

WHAT DO MEN WANT?

Men often take a different approach to health – they may be somewhat shyer about what they want to do – but here are some of the common requests I get from male clients.

- *More energy:* Just like women, men want to have more energy. You have to expend energy in order to get more and that is one of the reasons that this plan contains exercise. By reducing the amount of processed food in your diet and exercising more, you will dramatically increase the amount of energy you have.

- *Lose that beer belly:* One of the classic reasons for men wanting to lose weight – the hard beer belly that protrudes from shirts and T-shirts. This is caused by the yeast in beers and ciders that stays within the gut and ferments. This means that it expands and bloats out, resulting in the firm, round stomach that we all know. The good news is that you can make a big, big difference in a short space of time. Sometimes a colonic is recommended but generally a clean diet with plenty of fibre will do the trick.

- *Feel better:* The Slim Solution method is all about improving your life, using exercise and nutrition to kick-start your body back to its normal healthy state. One big benefit is that you will feel better.

You will feel alive, full of positivity and energy, ready to take on the world.

These are some of the most common goals that my clients have – I am sure many of them will resonate with you. You may also have your own goals, which are the reason you want to get started. Later in the book, I will show you a simple way to ensure you are working towards the right goals but now let's move on to something equally important: changing your habits!

2

CHECKLIST – BEFORE YOU START

ENERGY

LIFE

POWER

could give you lots more information about health, habits and everything else that I want to tell you, but I bet by now you just want to get started – you want to get healthy and don't want to waste any more time. So that's exactly what we are going to do: let's start the Slim Solution and get your health back!

However, it is important to ensure that it's safe for you to start the plan and that you have everything you need before you begin. As with all things, planning is key. So let's take a quick look through your health check and your pre-plan checklist.

PRE-PLAN HEALTH CHECK

Before starting this or any exercise programme, if

you have concerns about your ability to exercise you should always consult your GP. If you have any injuries prior to starting, please visit your local physiotherapist for advice. If you feel sick, dizzy or nauseous at any stage, stop exercising straight away. Ensure you are drinking plenty of water while exercising, sipping constantly during the session.

On the off chance that you acquire any injuries during the plan, the treatment is always the same: follow the R.I.C.E. technique.

- **Rest:** When you are injured you must stop exercising so that you can't do any further damage to the muscle, ligament or tendon. While it may be the hardest thing to do, it is probably the most important.

- **Ice:** Cold is a great way to reduce swelling and bruising and also improve circulation to the area of injury. Take a bag of ice or a bag of frozen vegetables, wrap a towel around it and place it on the injured area. Check for redness/ soreness every two minutes to ensure you aren't burning the skin. If you notice soreness, then don't apply any more ice.

- **Compression:** This aids recovery by keeping excess fluid away from the area and giving support when returning to exercising. Supports and compression clothing are available in local sports stores.

- **Elevation:** This is one of the simplest ways to avoid swelling. You need to sit down and keep the injured body part higher than the body – you can use a cushion or pillow to do this and also add support.

If you haven't exercised for some time, then don't jump in and overdo the exercise programme in this plan – ease into it at a level that suits you and gradually increase the intensity over time.

HEALTH QUESTIONNAIRE

Take a few minutes to fill in this simple questionnaire to ensure that it is safe for you to begin training. The questions below are intended as a guide to cover most medical issues. If you tick yes for any of the questions below, I recommend a checkup with your GP before you start.

Do you have now or have you ever had ... (please tick)	YES	NO
History of heart problems?		
High blood pressure?		
High cholesterol?		
Difficulty with physical exercise?		
Ligament, tendon or cartilage injury?		
Muscle/ joint/back disorder aggravated by physical activity?		
Chronic illness/taking medications?		
Allergies or hay fever?		
History of asthma, diabetes or epilepsy?		

	YES	NO
Have you had recent surgery (within last 6 months)?		
Is there a history of heart problems in the immediate family?		
Do you get chest pain during or after exercise?		
Do you feel out of breath at rest or after slight exertion?		
Are you pregnant or have you been pregnant in the last 4 months?		

GEAR CHECKLIST

Failing to plan is planning to fail, so it's essential to ensure you have everything you need before you start. Here is a simple list of what you will need to complete the exercise portion of the plan over the coming 30 days:

- Good pair of trainers (ask the shop to assess your gait when buying new runners)

- Rain jacket

- Four or five breathable T-shirts

- Two or three pairs of shorts/ tracksuit bottoms

- Five pairs of sports socks (light and breathable)

- Water bottle

- Exercise mat or towels

- Two 750 ml and one 1.5 litre bottles of water (as weights)

- Epsom salts (to help relieve any pain)

In chapter seven, you will find a list of useful kitchen essentials to help you get the most from the cooking and nutrition part of the plan.

YOUR COMMITMENT CONTRACT

Although you might be sceptical about them, commitment contracts are surprisingly effective. They provide a visible agreement to follow the 30-day method and can be helpful to keep you on track when you feel like giving up. So have a look below and fill in your contract. Take a picture with your phone and use it as your screen saver.

COMMITMENT CONTRACT

Date: _____

Name: _____

I commit to prioritising my health and myself over the next 30 days. I will follow the outlined 30-day plan and ensure that I work hard, eat healthily and put myself first for the next 30 days. I want to achieve the very best that I can and will strive to do just that.

Signed: _____

THE NEXT STEP: YOUR GOAL LIST

You are nearly there, nearly ready to start the plan, but first you have something important to do – something that so many people fail to do when trying to lose weight, get fit or change their lives. Identifying your real goals is crucial to getting the most out of the plan and helping you to achieve the very best that you can. Here is a quick process to help you to identify exactly what you want to accomplish over the coming month.

The first thing you need to do is a brain dump.

Take out an A4 pad a couple of hours before you go to bed and write down each and every goal that comes into your mind – it can be anything at all, just get it down on paper. Leave it there for an hour or two and clear your head. When you come back to it, you will be amazed at how the important things jump out.

Now take a different-coloured pen and circle the goals that are most important to you.

Write those goals down on another page and arrange them numerically so that you can clearly see the one that is most important to you.

It really is that simple: you now have your true goal, which will help to give you focus over the coming weeks.

YOUR PRE-PLAN MEASUREMENTS

Measurements are essential to track your progress. I want you to take your measurements on day one and then every seven days for the 30 days of the plan. The table gives simple guidelines for where to measure to ensure that the measurements will be consistent. Measure at the same time each week.

	Start	Week 1	Week 2	Week 3	Week 4
Weight (in lbs or kilos)					
Neck (in inches or cms)					
Right arm (widest point)					
Bust/Back (nipple line)					
Waist (belly button)					
Hips (widest point)					
Right leg (halfway point)					
Right calf (widest point)					

FINALLY, DON'T OVERTRAIN

This plan is built to help you change your life through exercise and nutrition. You may not have done exercise for some time and, for a very small percentage of people, this increases your risk of overtraining. Overtraining can be seriously bad for your body and it is important to be able to identify the common symptoms:

- Washed-out feeling, tired, drained, lack of energy

- Mild leg soreness, general aches and pains that don't go away after a few days

- Pain in muscles and joints

- Sudden drop in performance

- Insomnia

- Headaches

- Decreased immunity (increased number of colds and sore throats)

- Decrease in training capacity

- Moodiness and irritability

- Depression

- Loss of enthusiasm for exercise

- Decreased appetite

If you think that you are overtraining over the course of the 30 days, or at any time, the first thing to do is reduce or stop your exercise and take a few days' rest. Drink plenty of fluids and alter your diet if necessary by adding in extra protein foods, such as chicken or turkey, and some extra brown carbs. These nutrients will help you to recover as fast as possible.

There are several ways you can measure some signs of overtraining:

- Track your heart rate during training. If it is high and your effort level is low then you may be close to being overtrained.

- Track your resting heart rate each morning. Any marked increase from the norm may indicate that you aren't fully recovered and may need more rest.

You will know your body better than anyone else – if you begin to lose interest in your training and hate going out for the sessions then, chances are, you're close to being overtrained. Rest, glorious rest is the best medicine. Ease back into your training and try to ensure that you are eating the best nutrients possible to avoid it happening again.

3

THE 30-DAY PLAN

THINK

BELIEVE

ACHIEVE

You have written down your goals, filled in your health questionnaire and are motivated and ready to start changing your life. For the next 30 days I will become your personal trainer. The important thing is to follow the plan as I have laid it out, especially in terms of exercise. Don't try to do more sets or longer walks – I have built the plan specifically for optimum results and included rest days for a reason, so even if it seems too easy at the beginning, don't worry: it will become a little harder as you progress. Just follow each day and each page in turn and watch your body change. I have also included a section on post-workout stretches at the end of this chapter. Do them after each exercise session to help ensure you remain injury-free.

You will find 30 delicious breakfast, lunch and dinner recipes in chapter nine and all of these are designed for the plan. If you find something on the day-to-day plan in this chapter that isn't to your liking, you can simply change it for one of those recipes. If you are a vegetarian, you can substitute tofu or Quorn for the meat options in the recipes.

The lunches in the plan aren't overly complicated. I wanted to include foods that you can access easily and that won't be too different from what you may have eaten before. I believe that small changes such as switching white bread for brown will make a big difference to your health and the 30-day plan is going to show you that. Any salad options don't include mayonnaise-based salads.

In chapter eight I describe in greater detail my food philosophy, the importance of low-GI foods and managing your treat days. You might find it helpful to skip ahead and read this now so you can understand more about the Slim Solution food choices. But if not, there's enough information in the plan to get you started and help you through the 30 days. So let's begin!

DAY 1

FOOD

Breakfast: porridge made with skimmed milk

Snack 1: apple or kiwi

Lunch: brown-bread chicken-salad sandwich

Snack 2: handful of nuts

Dinner: brown pasta with quick tomato and olive sauce (p. 239)

EXERCISE

- **The squat:** Place your feet shoulder width apart, back straight and arms extended to the front. Simply bend your knees as far as you feel comfortable and return to the start. Do 20 reps and three sets altogether. Reps are just the number of times you need to do an exercise before taking a break and sets are the number of times you do the reps.

- **The lunge:** Start with your feet together, back straight. Now simply step forward with your right leg and bend your left knee towards the floor. Ensure the knee

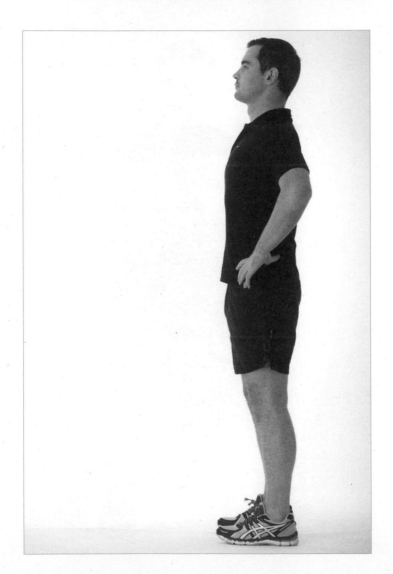

of the leading leg doesn't extend over your foot. Return to starting position. Repeat for 20 on the right leg and then 20 on the left. Do three sets in total.

- **The pullover:** This is one of the best exercises to stretch out the upper body and loosen your shoulders and back. Start by lying on your back on the floor with your knees bent. Using a 1.5 litre bottle of water as a weight, take it in both hands and straighten your arms towards the ceiling. While pushing your back into the floor and keeping your arms straight, lower your arms back towards the floor behind your head. Return to the centre. Aim for three sets of 20.

MOTIVATION

'*Your time is limited, so don't waste it living someone else's life*' – Steve Jobs.

CLIENT STORY: AILEEN

A few months ago, I decided to work with a personal trainer to create a suitable fitness and healthy-eating regime for myself. It's a decision I don't regret. With a positive attitude, hard work and determination, I've made some very positive changes to my life … and my waistline!

> *A few months on, I see fitness as fun. I actually miss it if I don't get my daily 'fitness fix' … The more exercise I do, the looser that Saturday-night dress is … How could anyone regret that?*

WORD OF THE DAY

Accomplish

DAY 2

FOOD

Breakfast: scrambled eggs made with three eggs – no butter, salt or milk

Snack 1: apple or orange

Lunch: vegetable soup with a slice of brown bread

Snack 2: handful of cashew nuts

Dinner: grilled steak with cherry tomato and mixed leaves (p. 237)

EXERCISE

Today is the cardio day so get your runners on and out for a 60-minute fast walk. You should be covering roughly four miles in this timeframe. To get the most out of your session when walking, you need to do three things:

- Maintain good posture, keeping your back straight

- Swing your arms by your sides to help you work faster

- Change your stride throughout the walk

You should never be fully out of breath – if you can hold a conversation at all times, you're doing it right.

MOTIVATION

'*Two roads diverged in a wood, and I –*
I took the one less travelled by,
and that has made all the difference'
– Robert Frost.

WORD OF THE DAY

Transform

EXPERT: PAULA MEE, NUTRITIONIST

What does health mean to you?
Health is so much more than what we eat and how much activity we get, I believe. To me, it means taking care of yourself – body, mind and spirit. That is striking the right balance between exercise, healthy eating, good sleep, spending time with those you love, feeling purposeful, staying positive and chocolate!

Being healthy does not include having a set of scales! It's about being comfortable in your own skin. So many of us are conditioned to see ourselves only through our weight or shape. Yet our shape is only one small part of who we are. Do you feel good, do you have plenty of energy, can you do the activities you want to do? That's what healthy living is all about, no matter what your weight is!

What would be your best piece of advice to someone who is starting to exercise?
No matter how slow you think you are going, you are still lapping everybody on the couch!

I think people new to exercise can make it a lot tougher on themselves. Keep it basic. Walking is one of the easiest (and cheapest) exercises you can get. Wearing a pedometer can add extra motivation by keeping you working towards a goal each day. Many people start with 5,000 steps or less and gradually build up to reaching 10,000–15,000 steps per day. People respond well to targets and this is a good way of getting you started.

What is your favourite treat?
A good cheeseboard, grapes, figs and apples and a really good red wine. Heaven!

Who is your sporting idol and why?
It has to be Katie Taylor. She is such an incredible ambassador for Ireland and a fantastic role model. I still remember where I was when she won gold in London – the whole country seemed to stop for her fight. And it couldn't have happened to a more grounded and down to earth person. She thoroughly deserved the Irish Sports Personality of the Year award and is a real inspiration to women, young and old. She is proof that if you fight hard enough, you can achieve your dream!

DAY 3

FOOD

Breakfast: bran flakes with skimmed milk

Snack 1: pineapple or kiwi

Lunch: turkey mixed salad with an oil-based dressing

Snack 2: handful of Brazil nuts

Dinner: baked sea bass with stir-fried vegetables (p. 240)

EXERCISE

Repeat exercises for Day 1.

MOTIVATION

'*If you can dream it, you can do it*' – Walt Disney.

WORD OF THE DAY

Commit

DAY 4

FOOD

Breakfast: two poached eggs with a slice of wholegrain toast

Snack 1: apple or orange

Lunch: hummus with two wholegrain Ryvita or carrot/cucumber sticks

Snack 2: handful of nuts and seeds

Dinner: brown pasta with quick tomato and olive sauce (p. 239)

EXERCISE

Get the runners back on today for a 60-minute fast walk. Try to cover a little more distance than on your first, ensuring that you're maintaining good posture all the way!

MOTIVATION

'*You miss 100% of the shots you don't take*'
– Wayne Gretzky.

WORD OF THE DAY

Conquer

EXPERT: RAY O'CONNOR, CONNEMARA MARATHON RACE ORGANISER

What does health mean to you?

Health is everything, really. If you don't have good health you cannot live life to the full.

I thought I was living a full life until 13 years ago but I quickly realised that my life was actually full of the wrong things ... I was smoking 30 cigarettes a day, working 18 hours a day and not playing the other six hours. Weekends weren't much better. I was a six-foot-two, ten-and-a-half-stone stress-head and simply a train wreck about to happen – something had to change quickly and I was the only one who could change it.

As a child I was fascinated with running but never really excelled in the sport. I was always the mid-packer who had ambitions to be better. I trained to run a marathon when I was fourteen or fifteen – I got as far as sixteen miles in training but soon figured out that girls were more fun to chase than 26.2 miles! But when it came to deciding how to change my lifestyle aged 30, running a marathon was the obvious choice. On 1 April 2000 I signed up to run the New York Marathon for Croí, the West of Ireland Heart Foundation. This decision changed everything.

Over the past 13 years I've run 132 marathons including the 'toughest foot-race on earth', the Marathon des Sables – a 100-mile road race – and I completed the challenge of 10 marathons in 10 days twice.

I loved running so much that I decided to integrate it into my work and I established the Connemara International Marathon, which is now a successful business that I get a huge amount of job satisfaction from.

My social life was non-existent – I don't like pubs – so it was an additional bonus when I founded Marathon Club Ireland and met lots of great people, many of whom have become close friends. So running not only made me physically fitter and mentally healthier but also gave my work–life balance more structure and opened up a completely new social life that gives everything so much more meaning. Anyone can change. It just takes a tiny bit more effort than staying the same. The important thing is to be decisive and do it now. The worst thing you can do is to do nothing.

What would be your best piece of advice to someone who is starting to exercise?

Starting out, you really need to focus on why you need to

exercise, set yourself a goal, visualise the effect of achieving the goal and taste the sense of achievement by giving yourself small milestones to reach along the way.

The most important thing when choosing a goal is to make it almost achievable. 'I might be able to walk 10K under 90 minutes' might seem crazy at the outset but when you break it down to a mini target of getting to 2K in 18 mins and build from there it doesn't seem as tough. One big goal and a set of mini targets along the way is the best way to keep focused on the task.

What is your favourite treat?

I seem to train best during the winter. As soon as November arrives I'm ready to take running seriously again. All the fun and games of the summer months are over and the brisk winter nights bring a lovely sense of calm. Unfortunately, all that calm is embraced by a biting cold. So my favourite treat is a hot bath after a long run in the cold. I have to admit, though, that in summer it's a cold beer! Well, hell, I deserve it!

Who is your sporting idol and why?

I have so many it's hard to pinpoint. I remember clearly the excitement across the country in 1976 during the Montreal Olympics when Eamonn Coghlan was building up to the

1,500 metres final. I have little doubt that I was the only kid in the country that was quietly rooting for my idol at the time, New Zealander John Walker. At just seven years old I was a huge fan of Walker and was thrilled to see him take gold. At the same time I remember being bitterly disappointed for Coghlan that he was pipped in the home straight for a bronze. It was a remarkable race for me to watch and one that influenced me immensely.

Ireland has some truly amazing sporting heroes: Sonia O'Sullivan, Ronnie Delaney, Catherina McKiernan, Eamonn Coghlan, Mick Molloy, John Treacy and the list goes on, each one hugely inspiring. But again, I'll buck the trend and look outside Ireland at my true idol, Czech runner Emil Zatopek, who has a remarkable story, highlighted in his exploits in the 1952 Olympics in Helsinki. After winning gold in the 5,000 and 10,000 metres, he decided at the last minute to take on the marathon, where he won his third gold. He was some man and is worth a google.

DAY 5

FOOD

Breakfast: low-sugar muesli and natural yoghurt

Snack 1: pineapple or kiwi

Lunch: mixed chicken salad with oil-based dressing

Snack 2: handful of nuts or seeds

Dinner: baked salmon with fennel (p. 240)

EXERCISE

Repeat exercises for Day 1.

MOTIVATION

'*I've missed more than 9,000 shots in my career. I've lost almost 300 games. 26 times I've been trusted to take the game winning shot and missed. I've failed over and over and over again in my life. And that is why I succeed'* – Michael Jordan.

WORD OF THE DAY

Act

» → DAY 6 ← «

FOOD

Breakfast: two boiled eggs (or three if you like – just leave out the yolk on the third)

Snack 1: strawberries or apple

Lunch: brown turkey-salad wrap

Snack 2: handful of Brazil nuts

Dinner: Japanese marinated beef with cucumber pickle (p. 245)

EXERCISE

Today is going to be your best cardio session yet. Tomorrow is a rest day so aim to walk even further than before – just ensure that the session is a 60-minute fast walk. Aim to cover four miles in the 60 minutes. Remember you should always be able to hold a conversation and never be fully out of breath.

MOTIVATION

'Every strike brings me closer to the next home run' – Babe Ruth.

WORD OF THE DAY

Victorious

What does health mean to you?
To be fit, illness free, sharp of mind and never tired and lacking in energy.

What would be your best piece of advice to someone who is starting to exercise?
See your programme as a long-term project. You are preparing to be healthy all your life – not just now. You are creating your future.

What is your favourite treat?
Steak and onions!

Who is your sporting idol and why?
Mark Pollock, who overcame many obstacles in his life and, despite being blind and disabled, conquered many gruelling challenges, and Katie Taylor who, with great faith and belief in herself, became an Olympic champion and a great inspiration to young people.

DAY 7

FOOD

Breakfast: your choice of any of the fabulous breakfasts in the recipe section

Snack 1: pineapple chunks

Lunch: choose from any of the lunch options in chapter nine

Snack 2: handful of cashew nuts

Dinner: this is your treat meal where you can have whatever you want in terms of your favourite foods – it could be pizza or a takeaway, but whatever it is you can enjoy it guilt free! Learn more about managing treats in chapter eight.

EXERCISE

There is no exercise to do today: your body has had a tough week so it's time to kick back, relax and recover. Things get a bit harder next week so enjoy your rest. Don't forget to do your second weigh-in today and take your measurements – compare them to day one.

MOTIVATION

'*We become what we think about*' – Earl Nightingale.

WORD OF THE DAY

Powerful

⟫→ DAY 8 ←⟪

FOOD

Breakfast: porridge with skimmed milk and honey

Snack 1: kiwi

Lunch: mixed tuna salad

Snack 2: handful of nuts

Dinner: grilled chicken and steamed green vegetables (p.242)

EXERCISE

- **Tricep dips:** These are one of my favourite exercises to tone up the backs of the arms, one of the parts of the body that trouble so many women. Start by sitting on the edge of a chair, hands on the seat by your hips, feet flat on the ground as far away from the body as possible. Lift your bum off and out from

75

the seat, bend elbows and lower towards the ground, then straighten your arms again. Try to do three sets of 20 reps.

- **Ski squats:** These are a simple but incredibly effective exercise for the whole lower body and the core. Start by placing your back against a wall and your feet out in front, shoulder width apart. Bend your knees and simply lower your body until your legs are parallel to the floor. Hold for as long as you feel comfortable.

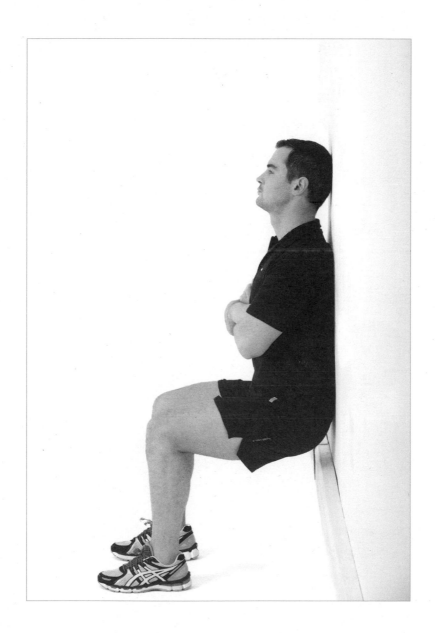

- **Press-ups:** It's time to work the upper body a little harder. Place your knees on the floor and your hands a little wider than shoulder width apart. Simply bend your arms and lower your chest to the floor, then straighten your arms again. Try three sets of 20.

MOTIVATION

'*Twenty years from now you will be more disappointed by the things that you didn't do than by the ones you did do, so throw off the bowlines, sail away from safe harbor, catch the trade winds in your sails. Explore, dream, discover*' – Mark Twain.

WORD OF THE DAY

Accomplish

FOOD

Breakfast: scrambled eggs with a slice of wholegrain toast

Snack 1: pineapple

Lunch: brown-bread turkey-salad sandwich

Snack 2: handful of cashew nuts

Dinner: grilled steak with cherry tomato and mixed leaves (p. 237)

EXERCISE

Now it's time to add some extra distance into your walks: the aim is to get over four miles in 60 minutes. Remember, you should be slightly out of breath but still able to hold a conversation.

MOTIVATION

'Don't wait. The time will never be just right'
– Napoleon Hill.

WORD OF THE DAY

Flourish

EXPERT: ALAN RYAN, IRONMAN TRIATHLETE

What does health mean to you?
It's a great privilege and not to be taken for granted. It's being able to chase my kids and the view from the top of a mountain.

What advice would you give to someone starting out?
Persevere: at first you may not enjoy it, but I promise in time you will. Soon you will be exercising for the simple pleasure of it and not just for the many benefits it brings.

What is your favourite treat?
Indian takeaway.

Who is your sporting idol and why?
Dick Hoyt – well, actually Dick and Rick Hoyt: they are a team. I couldn't possibly do them justice trying to describe their sporting achievements. I recommend the reader search them out on YouTube. You will be richly rewarded with a story of true sportsmanship and not the regretfully all-too-familiar fairytale of elite sport.

»→ DAY 10 ←«

FOOD

Breakfast: bran flakes with skimmed milk

Snack 1: apple or orange

Lunch: vegetable soup

Snack 2: handful of nuts

Dinner: choose from one of your favourite recipes so far

EXERCISE

Repeat exercises for Day 8.

MOTIVATION

'*Winning isn't everything, but wanting to win is*' – Vince Lombardi.

WORD OF THE DAY

Concentrate

DAY 11

FOOD

Breakfast: two poached eggs with a slice of brown toast

Snack 1: pineapple

Lunch: mixed chicken salad with oil-based dressing

Snack 2: handful of nuts

Dinner: halibut with rocket salad and grilled courgettes (p. 244)

EXERCISE

Today's exercise is a 60-minute fast walk. Each walk that you do should be faster and further than the previous one, so don't be afraid to push the body a bit harder.

MOTIVATION

'Whether you think you can or you think you can't, you're right' – Henry Ford.

WORD OF THE DAY

Energize

EXPERT: LOUIS BOWEN, LONDON-BASED PERSONAL TRAINER

What does health mean to you?
Health, to me, means you are continuously looking for ways to better yourself.

- Feeling stronger, more focused and happier in both body and mind and attempting to be the best 'you' you can be.
- Discipline and regime, incorporating both exercise and nutrition, in one's everyday life.
- See your world as a gym/assault course. Walk to work if possible; allow time for the gym or an exercise class. Allow time to stretch and relax.
- Learn about diet. Enjoy eating. Improve your vitality and wellbeing with every meal. Once a week reward your hard work with a cheat day. Eat and do whatever you like. Balance and enjoyment is the key to a healthy life.

What would be your best piece of advice to someone who is starting to exercise?

Obviously if you have any doubts see your doctor. If you're new to exercise start gently – for me or my clients I always use the maxim 'Crawl, Walk, Run'. By doing so you will safely and constructively teach your body 'new tricks', building on these over time. Every exercise or sport has progressions to be made: you will get there – just enjoy your journey and be patient. It will come!

What is your favourite treat?

A slice of chocolate cake (lots of icing) with a scoop of vanilla ice-cream.

Who is your sporting idol and why?

Damien Walters, free runner. Incorporating gymnastics into his movements, he demonstrates the extremes of what the human body is capable of.

»—→ DAY 12 ←—«

FOOD

Breakfast: low-sugar muesli and natural yoghurt with honey

Snack 1: apple or orange

Lunch: smoked salmon on wholegrain Ryvita

Snack 2: handful of cashew nuts

Dinner: baba ganoush (p. 245)

EXERCISE

Repeat exercises for Day 8.

MOTIVATION

'*The only person you are destined to become is the person you decide to be*' – Ralph Waldo Emerson.

WORD OF THE DAY

Encourage

»→ DAY 13 ←«

FOOD

Breakfast: two boiled eggs

Snack 1: some pineapple or a kiwi

Lunch: chunky vegetable soup

Snack 2: handful of nuts

Dinner: Japanese marinated beef with cucumber pickle (p. 245)

EXERCISE

Today's exercise is your last 60-minute fast walk for this week. Tomorrow is the rest day so really put in a big effort today!

MOTIVATION

'*Believe you can and you're halfway there*'
– Theodore Roosevelt.

WORD OF THE DAY

Dream

EXPERT: JEN FEIGHERY, PERSONAL TRAINER

What does health mean to you?
I believe health is a combination of both your physical and mental states of wellbeing. Feeding your mind with positive thoughts, exercising the body and eating nutritious foods are all important in the creation of a healthy life.

What would be your best piece of advice to someone who is starting to exercise?
It's very important to set yourself various short-term goals which will lead you to achieving your overall long-term goal. For example, losing two to three stone initially will seem impossible to you, but if you create weekly short-term goals these will build up and lead you to achieving the big one. Using the SMART method is a good place to start when goal setting.

- *Specific:* be specific with what you want to achieve and to what extent
- *Measurable:* track your progress and measure the outcome, e.g. food diary, training diary, weekly weigh-in

- *Attainable:* setting out goals that will eventually be achieved
- *Realistic:* initially your goals should appear optimistic and challenging; however it's important to ensure the goals are realistic and not too extreme (exercising twice a day for seven days is not realistic)
- *Timely:* include a time limit. By when? Having a couple of events to work towards is great for keeping you motivated and getting you out the door to exercise (e.g. wedding, race, holidays, birthdays)

What is your favourite treat?
It's a toss up between pizza and banoffee (Avoca banoffee is to die for)!

Who is your sporting idol and why?
Jessica Ennis – she is a fantastic role model for females all around the world. I love how she didn't allow her setbacks to prevent her from going on to achieve her dream of winning an Olympic gold medal in London 2012. She is living proof that you can achieve anything you want through determination, dedication and hard work.

 DAY 14

FOOD

Breakfast: your choice of any of the breakfasts in the recipe section

Snack 1: pineapple chunks

Lunch: choose from any of the lunch options in chapter nine

Snack 2: handful of cashew nuts

Dinner: long-term health is all about balance, so today is your day to have your treat meal: savour it and enjoy it.

EXERCISE

I have given you harder exercises this week so it's essential to let your body recover: take it easy today and relax. Don't forget to weigh-in again and measure up.

MOTIVATION

'Once you choose hope, anything's possible'
– Christopher Reeve.

WORD OF THE DAY

Pride

CLIENT STORY: SARAH

I can stand here and say legitimately and honestly that I am the healthiest I have ever been. I'm at my target weight, I am running faster than I ever have before and I've even taken up sprint triathlons. I'm buying clothes I like rather than those that just fit. I feel confident, positive, happy and strong. I've taken the plunge and left my job of 15 years to embark on a new and exciting adventure doing what I really want to do. Who said this was all about physique and how I look? A healthy body is a healthy mind! I would have achieved none of this if it weren't for the hard work I put in and the support I got to get healthy. I am truly fit and feel positive and mentally strong. I sum it all up in one word – healthy.

DAY 15

FOOD

Breakfast: porridge with skimmed milk and honey

Snack 1: strawberries

Lunch: brown-bread turkey-salad sandwich

Snack 2: handful of nuts

Dinner: baked sea bass with stir-fried vegetables (p. 240)

EXERCISE

Today we are going to push the body a bit further with four exercises in total.

- **Wide-foot squat:** Start with the feet wider than shoulder width apart and facing away from the body. Bend your knees and lower your bum towards the floor and hold. Now simply further

lower your bum three–four inches and back up. Repeat for 20 and do three sets.

- **Tricep dips:** See p. 75. Repeat for three sets of 20 reps.

- **The lunge:** See p. 54. Do three sets of 20 in total.

- **Pec deck:** Start with your feet shoulder width apart and hold your two 750ml water bottles in your hands. Bring your arms up so that your elbows are in line with your shoulders. Simply touch the base of the elbows together in the centre and return to the side. Try for three sets of 20. (Images overleaf)

MOTIVATION

'*When one door of happiness closes, another opens, but often we look so long at the closed door that we do not see the one that has been opened for us*' – Helen Keller

WORD OF THE DAY

Congratulate

EXPERT: HEATHER IRVINE, MODEL, HEALTH JOURNALIST AND ADRENALINE JUNKIE

What does health mean to you?

Health to me is happiness. If you eat well and get out there and exercise you will feel fantastic, have buckets more energy and be able to cram so much more into your day.

What would be your best piece of advice to someone who is starting to exercise?

Don't ever think, I can't do that. Choose activities that are enjoyable so it won't be a chore and team up with a buddy. Then set yourselves a goal and go for it. Nothing feels as satisfying as crossing the finish line of your first race or running your first 10K. I guarantee you will be pleasantly surprised by what you are capable of.

What is your favourite treat?

My friend Clodagh makes the most divine flapjacks – they are utterly sinful but, balanced out with lots of seeds (or so I like to think), they are a brilliant energy source when you are out on the hills and equally tasty with a cup of tea after a hard training session. It is all about rewards!

Who is your sporting idol and why?

Stephen Redmond is my sporting idol. When he first said he was going to swim around the Fastnet, people told him he would never do it. He proved them wrong and then he went on to swim the seven oceans last year, becoming the first person in the world to do so. He never hides how tough the challenges are but instead looks straight into the face of the impossible and makes it possible. When presented with a challenge the question should never be why but rather why not!

» → DAY 16 ← «

FOOD

Breakfast: scrambled eggs with a slice of wholegrain toast

Snack 1: pineapple

Lunch: hummus with wholegrain Ryvita

Snack 2: handful of nuts

Dinner: brown pasta with quick tomato and olive sauce (p. 239)

EXERCISE

It's time for a one-hour fast walk. You should be covering at least four miles within the hour and even a little further if possible. Don't be afraid to try different routes, as this can make a big difference.

MOTIVATION

'*Everything has beauty, but not everyone can see*'
– Confucius.

WORD OF THE DAY

Empower

»→ DAY 17 ←«

FOOD

Breakfast: bran flakes with skimmed milk and berries

Snack 1: apple or orange

Lunch: smoked salmon on wholegrain Ryvita

Snack 2: handful of nuts

Dinner: chicken breast with ratatouille (p.237)

EXERCISE

Repeat exercises for Day 15.

MOTIVATION

'*How wonderful it is that nobody need wait a single moment before starting to improve the world*'
– Anne Frank.

WORD OF THE DAY

Love

EXPERT: NEIL O'BRIEN, TRIATHLETE AND NUTRITIONIST

What does health mean to you?
It's a lot more than just being free of illness or disease. To me it's about not being compromised by factors that are within your control — whether that's having the ability to do your daily activities, work-related, playing football with your kids, taking out the bins or going for a swim.

What would be your best piece of advice to someone who is starting to exercise?
Pick something that you like, whether it's running, salsa dancing, cycling or volleyball. You are more likely to stick at it when tired, as we are in this for the long haul! Also availing of the social or competitive element of sports or hobbies can make exercise more interesting.

What is your favourite treat?
Whipped cream and chocolate.

Who is your sporting idol and why?

Murray O'Donnell, triathlete. He's not a well-known sportsperson but I saw him compete at the world age-group championship (60–64 category): he was in first place with only 5K to go. He collapsed and was brought to the medical tent, all the while thinking he was in second place. Afterwards when he was told that he was actually leading the race he just laughed and said he only came for first place and was happy that he'd pushed that hard. He never once complained about the medal he lost. That is true sportsmanship and what it taught me is that it's about the process, not the outcome.

DAY 18

FOOD

Breakfast: two poached eggs with a slice of wholegrain toast

Snack 1: kiwi

Lunch: vegetable soup

Snack 2: handful of nuts

Dinner: turkey escalope with tomato salsa and green salad (p.236)

EXERCISE

Time to hit the road again today with a one-hour fast walk. As always, try to push the body a little harder.

MOTIVATION

'*When I let go of what I am, I become what I might be*' – Lao Tzu.

WORD OF THE DAY

Persevere

CLIENT STORY: JANE

I started training with Karl a year ago. In school I had been very sporty and was always full of energy. However in my twenties I had stopped doing any kind of exercise and only really broke a sweat the odd Saturday night dancing! I needed a kick-start to get my fitness up and get me moving again. After I got past the initial sore muscles from my first few training sessions, I began to feel really energised and would look forward to my next session. I had not expected to see results so quickly but within the first four weeks the classes and sessions became more enjoyable and I lost inches from around my waist.

The biggest benefit for me has been developing an awareness about my body: I breathe deeper than before, I stand straighter and I feel stronger. If I'm stressed about work or my mood is low, I can change that by working out for an hour. When I decided to embrace exercise it seemed like just another decision – a year later it has become an integral part of my life and I'll never look back.

»→ DAY 19 ←«

FOOD

Breakfast: low-sugar muesli with natural yoghurt and honey

Snack 1: apple or orange

Lunch: mixed tuna salad with oil-based dressing

Snack 2: handful of Brazil nuts

Dinner: choose from one of your favourite recipes so far

EXERCISE

Repeat exercises for Day 15.

MOTIVATION

'*The difference between a successful person and others is not lack of strength, not a lack of knowledge but rather a lack of will*' – Vince Lombardi.

WORD OF THE DAY

Live

EXPERT: MAURICE WHELAN, EXECUTIVE COACH

What does health mean to you?
Health to me is a feeling of wellbeing in the mind as well as the body. If I take body, it's a feeling of energy and wellness I get from eating well and exercising. To get a healthy body, it's about consistency and committing to changing how I eat and exercise to ensure I am giving my body the best chance to do its best for me. If I look at people who have maintained their weight and health it was never through fad or quick-fix diets: it was always by committing to and sticking to a healthy exercise and eating plan.

What would be your best piece of advice to someone who is starting to exercise?
Start now! We are all great at starting at some time in the future – how many times have we said, I'll start on Monday, after the holidays, on the first of January? Encourage a friend to go on the health adventure with you. That way you can back each other up and pull each other along mentally when you hit a brick wall. I have a fantastic friend, Ellen, who I have trained with for over six years now, and we even

did a triathlon together. It's great to have someone in your corner. When you commit to meeting someone at the gym, or for that walk or swim, it makes it that much harder to sit on the couch when you are feeling wrecked from looking after the kids all day, or exhausted from a day at work.

What is your favourite treat?

I have to say my favourite treat is a pot of Rachel's Organic Greek Style Coconut Bio-live Yogurt. I just love it. When I'm having a dessert, the fact it's organic and bio-live means that as desserts go it's not all bad! The taste is just fantastic and it's sweet ... So if you have a bit of a sweet tooth like me it ticks the boxes.

Who is your sporting idol and why?

My spodols are Dick and Rick Hoyt. Every time I am looking for inspiration I re-read their story or I watch their story on YouTube. Rick was born in 1962 to Dick and Judy Hoyt. Because of a lack of oxygen to the brain at the time of his birth, Rick was diagnosed as a spastic quadriplegic with cerebral palsy. Dick and his wife began a lifetime's work in a quest for Rick's inclusion in community, sports and education and challenged the world to see beyond Rick's physical limitations. His parents taught him the alphabet and basic words. In 1972 a group of engineers from Tufts

University developed an interactive computer that enabled Rick to communicate for the first time.

In the spring of 1977, Rick told his dad that he wanted to participate in a five-mile charity run. Dick agreed to run the five miles and push Rick in the wheelchair. After completing the race, Rick told his father, 'Dad, when I'm running, it feels like I'm not handicapped.' This realisation was just the beginning of what would become over a thousand races, including marathons, duathlons and triathlons (six of them ironman competitions). In a triathlon, for the swimming stage, Dick would pull Rick in a boat with a bungee cord attached to his waist and to the front of the boat. For the bike stage, Dick and Rick would ride a special two-seater bike, and then Dick would push Rick in his custom-made wheelchair for the running stage.

»→ DAY 20 ←«

FOOD

Breakfast: two boiled eggs

Snack 1: pineapple

Lunch: smoked salmon on wholegrain Ryvita

Snack 2: handful of cashew nuts

Dinner: grilled steak with cherry tomato and mixed leaves (p. 237)

EXERCISE

One-hour fast walk – today is the last walk of this week with a rest day coming tomorrow so let's really work hard and walk the furthest yet!

MOTIVATION

'*The only way of finding the limits of the possible is by going beyond them into the impossible*'
– Arthur C. Clarke.

WORD OF THE DAY

Overcome

CLIENT STORY: MARIAN

What I want to say to anyone starting out on this fitness and health plan is: you won't regret it. Take it from me – if I can do it, so can you. I was in my mid-forties before I finally took my health into my own hands. I had brilliant support from my family and friends, but did any of us really believe what would happen? I'm not so sure. I was never the sporty type – and as anyone around me knows, I've always liked my grub. The results have spoken for themselves though. And I still like my grub – but I know now when to stop eating, and happily, I know how good it feels to fit into a size 12 dress for the first time in 20 years – from a size 18 just one year ago!

DAY 21

FOOD

Breakfast: your choice of any of the breakfasts in the recipe section

Snack 1: apple

Lunch: choose from any of the lunch options in chapter nine

Snack 2: handful of cashew nuts

Dinner: treat day today – always my favourite – so pick a meal you have been craving and make sure you enjoy it!

EXERCISE

There is no exercise to do today – your body has had a tough week so it's time to relax and recover. Things will get harder again next week so enjoy your rest! Today is also your weigh-in day so don't forget.

MOTIVATION

'*If the wind will not serve, take to the oars*'
– Latin proverb.

WORD OF THE DAY

Be

EXPERT: GERRY DUFFY, MOTIVATIONAL SPEAKER

What does health mean to you?
All of us want to live a long and healthy life. Health is the condition of our body and mind. Our bodies are the vehicle through which we live out our standard of health, be it good or not so good. I believe we have a significant responsibility and a major role in determining its quality and longevity. We can contribute hugely to the excellence of this health 'condition' by the quality of food we eat and in the amount of physical exercise that we challenge our bodies to do. Whether we give them the credit for it or not, our bodies are paying attention every minute of every day. Embracing the philosophy that all of us can be an elite athlete in this regard will, I believe, contribute to a longer and healthier life. This is a great goal for us all to have in our lives.

What would be your best piece of advice to someone who is starting to exercise?
Find a form of physical activity that you enjoy. Many people take up running, cycling, walking or whatever because they see others being active and they want to do something for themselves. The enthusiasm to do the same activity might last but it may not either. By doing some form of activity that you love to do, you are far more likely to keep it up.

What is your favourite treat?

An Indian meal with a glass of red wine. It must be earned, though, by eating well and exercising throughout the week.

Who is your sporting idol and why?

Terry Fox, the Canadian runner who died in 1981, is one of my absolute heroes. In 1980, having defeated a bout of cancer, Fox took to the Canadian highways and began to run across that country (3,000 miles) with the ambition to raise CAD$1M for cancer research. Sadly the disease returned when he was halfway across and silenced this inspirational teenager forever. His legacy lives on, though, and has since raised in excess of CAD$20M. I think about him often when I am training. By doing so I am motivated to make the most of this gift called life. He also has inspired me to pursue big sporting ambitions out of which I get so much enjoyment.

DAY 22

FOOD

Breakfast: porridge with skimmed milk and honey

Snack 1: apple or orange

Lunch: chunky vegetable soup

Snack 2: handful of nuts

Dinner: Japanese marinated beef with cucumber pickle (p. 245)

EXERCISE

This week it's going to get a little tougher again, with six exercises in total.

- **Bridge**: Start by lying on your front with your elbows on the floor, hands pointing away from you. Point your feet so you're resting on your toes. Keeping your back and legs straight, raise your body off the ground. Hold for as long as feels comfortable.

- **Tricep dips:** See p. 75.

- **The squat:** See p. 51.

- **The pullover:** See p. 56.

- **Ski squat:** See p. 77.

- **Bicep curls:** Start with your feet shoulder width apart and your back straight. Keeping your elbows by your sides, and using two 750ml water bottles as weights, bring the bottles up to your shoulders and back down. Aim for three sets and 20 reps of all the exercises. (Images overleaf)

MOTIVATION

'*You can't fall if you don't climb. But there's no joy in living your whole life on the ground*' – Unknown.

WORD OF THE DAY

Laugh

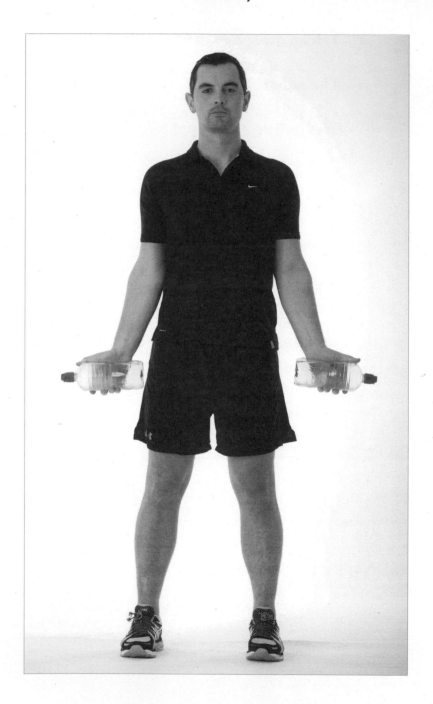

DAY 23

FOOD

Breakfast: scrambled eggs with a slice of wholegrain toast

Snack 1: pineapple

Lunch: hummus with wholegrain Ryvita

Snack 2: handful of Brazil nuts

Dinner: halibut with rocket salad and grilled courgettes (p. 244)

EXERCISE

Get your runners on and out you go for a one-hour fast walk. As always, aim to walk faster and a little further as you get fitter.

MOTIVATION

'Too many of us are not living our dreams because we are living our fears' – Les Brown.

WORD OF THE DAY

Breathe

CLIENT STORY: MARY

Shopping had become an increasingly dreaded experience, moving up dress sizes and buying loose clothes to conceal my larger body shape. The weight had crept on slowly: I made continual excuses for it and put off addressing the situation, always blaming my lack of time when in fact fear was the underlying factor.

My first meeting with Karl was an anxious and exciting experience. Having never been particularly fit and having a few health issues, I was nervous of failure. Karl was non-judgemental and believed in my ability, setting realistic and achievable challenges for me that required hard work and persistence. As my journey progressed, my confidence, determination and motivation increased.

Karl was always available with a friendly smile, offering words of encouragement at every opportunity. I reached my target by making the right choices and I continue to work out with Karl regularly. Healthy eating and regular exercise have become my way of life and I encourage everybody else to make them theirs too — I promise you won't regret it!

→ DAY 24 ←

FOOD

Breakfast: bran flakes with skimmed milk and berries

Snack 1: pineapple

Lunch: mixed chicken salad with oil-based dressing

Snack 2: handful of cashew nuts

Dinner: Karl's superfood vegetable soup (p. 246)

EXERCISE

Repeat exercises for Day 22.

MOTIVATION

'Challenges are what make life interesting and overcoming them is what makes life meaningful'
– Joshua J. Marine.

WORD OF THE DAY

Hope

CLIENT STORY: TOM

It was my kids that motivated me first to get fit. There's nothing worse than realising that you don't have it in you to run around chasing them and them screaming at you to play – that was hard. I'd put on a lot of weight over the years – liked my fries too much, got out of the habit of exercise. I knew it wasn't good but . . . anyway, the decision to get healthy again was the best I ever made. I followed Karl's plan for four months now and I can honestly say I feel 20 years younger. The biggest surprise of all – I don't even miss the fries! And as for the kids – how could I ever go back to how I was? Now I'm able to be the dad I always wanted to be. And I'm living by example, which has to be good for us all.

DAY 25

FOOD

Breakfast: two poached eggs with one slice of wholegrain toast

Snack 1: apple or orange

Lunch: mixed tuna salad with oil-based dressing

Snack 2: handful of nuts

Dinner: Thai chicken and brown noodle broth (p. 243)

EXERCISE

Today is another cardiovascular day, so out you get for a one-hour fast walk, setting another personal best in terms of distance and time.

MOTIVATION

'*The way to get started is to quit talking and begin doing*' – Walt Disney.

WORD OF THE DAY: Inspire

EXPERT: DR EDDIE MURPHY, CLINICAL PSYCHOLOGIST

What does health mean to you?
Health means 'healthy mind – healthy body', getting the balance right between living a life with energy, vitality and positivity on one hand, and with integrity, where you are true to yourself and others, on the other.

What would be your best piece of advice to someone who is starting to exercise?
If you want your life to change, your choices must change and today is the best day of your life to begin. Visualise your endpoint and set short, medium and long term goals to achieve it. Remember the difference between try and triumph is a little 'umph'!

What is your favourite treat?
Taytos – cheese and onion, deadly!

Who is your sporting idol and why?
My father. He regales me with stories of GAA matches he played in, of handball, boxing and running. At 79 years he is still coaching an under-14 team this year! And why is he my hero? Because he taught me that sport was about participation regardless of level: it gives life lessons of passion, friendship, loyalty, highs, lows, health, teamwork, perseverance, humility, community and spirit.

→ DAY 26 ←

FOOD

Breakfast: low-sugar muesli and natural yoghurt

Snack 1: kiwi

Lunch: turkey mixed salad with oil-based dressing

Snack 2: handful of nuts

Dinner: baked sea bass with stir-fried vegetables (p. 240)

EXERCISE

One-hour fast walk on a hilly route, pushing the body a little harder than before.

MOTIVATION

'*Expose yourself to your deepest fear; after that, fear has no power, and the fear of freedom shrinks and vanishes. You are free*' – Jim Morrison.

WORD OF THE DAY

Prioritise

CLIENT STORY: MARTIN

Feeling fit is awesome. In the past six months, I've traded hangovers for runs, and fast food for real food. I'm doing better at work, have way more energy, and even feel in a different mental space. As I said, awesome! It wasn't easy to start. I put it off for years really preferring to just go out and enjoy myself and eat what I wanted when I wanted and to hell with the consequences. Karl's plan has helped me get to a better place in my life, and I'm not planning on going back to where I was any time soon.

»→ DAY 27 ←«

FOOD

Breakfast: two boiled eggs with a slice of wholegrain toast

Snack 1: apple or orange

Lunch: smoked salmon on wholegrain Ryvita

Snack 2: handful of nuts

Dinner: turkey escalope with tomato salsa and green salad (p. 236)

EXERCISE

One-hour fast walk on a flat route, extending your stride and using all the fitness that you have gained!

MOTIVATION

'*You can't use up creativity. The more you use, the more you have*' – Maya Angelou.

WORD OF THE DAY

Aspire

EXPERT: ASH MAGUIRE, PERSONAL TRAINER

What does health mean to you?
There is a popular saying that your health is your wealth and it's absolutely true. Too often it is neglected in pursuit of other goals, our workload, career paths, family responsibilities and so on, but nothing is more important. To carry out these tasks to the best of our ability we need to have a healthy body and mind. Your health is everything, so treat it as such.

What would be your best piece of advice to someone who is starting to exercise?
Enjoy it. Too often our focus is on the image before us or on the scale below us. It is something I see every day through work and only serves to hold us back. We focus so much on this one outcome that we fail to appreciate the immediate outcome of the session in hand and its ultimate result — feeling good about ourselves. It's not about how we look, it's about how we feel, and I can guarantee you that after a tough workout session you will feel great, you will feel

strong, you will feel confident and you will feel like nothing or nobody can stop you. And that's really what exercise is all about.

What is your favourite treat?
Coffee and cream in the mornings – heaven.

Who is your sporting idol and why?
I grew up playing sports and always had a profound respect for the coaches who trained me. Behind every great athlete is a great coach and in secondary school, at Lumen Christi College, I was lucky enough to have two pivotal mentors – Suzanne Deery and Paula Fleming. Together, these girls helped me discover my passion for sport and physical fitness, encouraging me to reach new sporting heights and inspiring me by example to follow in their coaching footsteps. Their guidance and leadership had a lasting impact on my younger self and I too made it my mission in life to help and inspire others through the awesome power of physical fitness.

DAY 28

FOOD

Breakfast: porridge with skimmed milk and honey

Snack 1: pineapple

Lunch: chunky vegetable soup

Snack 2: handful of nuts

Dinner: grilled chicken and steamed green vegetables (p. 242)

EXERCISE

You are nearly there now, so let's push for one extra-long fast walk today: 90 minutes, at least six miles. It's a big challenge but one I know you can achieve – get your runners on and off you go!

MOTIVATION

'*Dream big and dare to fail*' – Norman Vaughan.

WORD OF THE DAY

Learn

CLIENT STORY: HARRY

From very young I was overweight. Fat. I felt it worse than ever in school where I was always getting slagged. I was glad to finish school. But I was still fat, more than ever. I'd always tried, everyone knew that. But nothing ever seemed to last and I'd be back to how I was before long. When I first started to follow Karl's method, I thought it would be the same but it wasn't. I just took it one day at a time – and the treat days really helped because before that's where I'd fall down, it was all or nothing. Now I could still have a treat, and it wasn't the end of the world. In fact it motivated me. I won't look back now. I've lost three stone in six months and though I may be much less the man I used to be in weight, I'm twice the man I was in confidence!

DAY 29

FOOD

Breakfast: scrambled eggs with a slice of wholegrain toast

Snack 1: apple or orange

Lunch: brown turkey-salad wrap

Snack 2: handful of Brazil nuts

Dinner: baked salmon with fennel (p. 240)

EXERCISE

One-hour fast walk, and the final one of the 30-day plan, so really go for it today!

MOTIVATION

'It's not the years in your life that count. It's the life in your years' – Abraham Lincoln.

WORD OF THE DAY

Create

EXPERT: SHANE M^CSHEA, PERSONAL TRAINER

What does health mean to you?

For me, health is the ability to do what you want when you want to and not be held back by a lack of confidence in your physical capabilities! Health is more than just looking good physically, as I've seen a lot of people grow hugely in many areas including confidence, motivation and happiness as their fitness progresses.

What would be your best piece of advice to someone who is starting to exercise?

Get started! Too many people tend to wait until the perfect time to get going but if you start now and focus on building even one new habit a fortnight over a 12-month period, that is 26 new habits and a huge amount of improvement!

What is your favourite treat?

Chocolate fudge cake and ice-cream.

Who is your sporting idol and why?

My parents. Dad (Pauric) had a successful Gaelic football career, which included captaining Donegal to an Ulster Championship, and both himself and my mum (Bregeen) played a massive part in developing my passion for fitness, from giving me endless lifts to football matches to encouraging us all to be as active and healthy as possible!

→→ DAY 30 ←←

You have made it! It's been a tough 30 days but well done for completing it and on your results. Today is your final day so you have your choices as usual and don't forget to weigh-in and measure too.

FOOD

Breakfast: your choice of any of the breakfasts in the recipe section

Snack 1: pineapple

Lunch: choose from any of the lunch options in chapter nine

Snack 2: handful of cashew nuts

Dinner: this is your treat meal so have whatever you want in terms of your favourite foods – it could be pizza or a takeaway, but whatever it is, enjoy it guilt free!

EXERCISE

You've done it – the final day! Over the past 30 days you have made big changes that will help you to stay healthy for the rest of your life. For today, I want you to pick your favourite five exercises from the last 30 days and do three sets of 20 of them – enjoy!

MOTIVATION

'If you can dream it, you can achieve it' – Zig Ziglar.

WORD OF THE DAY

Pride

Finally …

The past 30 days have helped to change your life. Eating healthier and adding some simple exercise into your life has shown you just what a difference this can make, so it's important to continue eating well and exercising in the future – find a sport that you enjoy and keep releasing those endorphins that have helped to change your life. You can keep using these exercises or, now that you have the foundations and the confidence in your body, try new ones. Go, reach for the stars and achieve all you can!

STRETCHES

The best stretches to do after your workout are static stretches. A static stretch is when you place your body in a certain position and flex a certain muscle group for 30 seconds or longer. Stretching after exercise will not only improve recovery but will also improve flexibility and reduce the risk of injury. Here are the top stretches.

- **Quadriceps:** These are the large muscles in the front of your upper leg. To stretch these, hold onto a chair or the wall with your right hand and bend your left knee, bringing your heel towards your bum. Hold your left foot in your left hand, pushing the foot in until you feel the stretch. Hold for a minimum of 30 seconds.

- **Hamstrings:** These are the muscles on the back of your upper leg. To stretch these, first lie down on your back and have both legs flat on the ground. Now lift one leg up, keeping it totally straight and your toe pointed toward your face. Grab that leg just above the knee joint and hold it in place, keeping the leg straight up. Hold for at least 30 seconds. Tip – use a belt or towel to pull your leg in, wrapping it around the foot and drawing it in slowly until you feel the stretch.

- **Calves:** These muscles on the lower part of your leg can get extremely tight after long runs. First stand several feet away from a wall and place one foot forward. Lean in to the wall and push your hands against it, keeping the heel of your back foot firmly on the ground. Keep your hip and head in a straight line and hold this pose for 30 seconds before switching legs.

- **Glutes:** This is a great stretch for your bum and is performed by first lying down on a mat or comfortable surface with the soles of your feet flat on the floor, knees bent. Next you are going to place your right ankle on your left knee, place your hands around the back of the left leg and pull it in towards your chest. Hold for 30 seconds and switch legs.

- **Inner thigh/groin:** To begin this stretch, first place your feet wide apart and then squat down, straightening your right leg out to the side as you slowly go down into the pose. Keep your hands on the ground for support or hold your right toes with your right hand. Move your hips until you are getting the full stretch for your inner thigh and hold for 30 seconds before switching sides.

TIPS FOR SUCCESS

1. If you have a busy schedule, start your day with an early-morning workout – you are less likely to make excuses if you get it done before something else can get in your way!

2. Share your goals with others – this is a great way to hold yourself accountable for taking action. It will give you greater purpose and help create a support network of family and friends.

3. You cannot out-train a bad diet – there is no point undoing all your hard work and effort by making poor

food choices. Commit to a diet of clean food and your training will improve immensely.

4. If you want to eat less, chew slowly and put down your knife and fork between mouthfuls. By simply savouring every bite we eat we can learn to appreciate food and not abuse it.

5. One pound of muscle is denser and smaller than one pound of fat. But they are not the same thing, fat doesn't turn to muscle and vice versa.

6. Plan ahead – preparation is key when it comes to both exercise and nutrition.

Have your foods prepared the night before and your workouts scheduled in advance: this way you are more committed and will not make poor food choices when on the go.

7. If nothing changes, then nothing changes. Look at your current nutrition and lifestyle choices and see if they are taking you down the right track to achieving your goal. If not, then what must you do to get on the right one?

8. Reflect daily – at the end of each day spend 10 minutes reflecting on the day's events, asking yourself what went well and what

needs improvement. Look at every aspect, from your work to exercise routine – how can you make it better tomorrow?

9. Limit your alcohol intake on nights out by setting limits for yourself and sticking to them, alternating with non-alcoholic drinks and drinking slowly with plenty of ice in your glass.

10. When you're having meat, choose lean cuts from your local butcher and cut off any visible fat before cooking. Meat is high in protein so consume post-training to help your muscles repair.

PHASE TWO

4

NOW IT'S TIME TO START THE REST OF YOUR LIFE

REJUVENATE

REGENERATE

RESCUE

Congratulations on completing the 30 days of the Slim Solution. It is amazing what you can achieve in such a short space of time and it is the perfect timeframe to help you to break a habit, which is one of the keys to long-term change. If you can get through the 30 days, I know from my personal experience with clients that you stand a greater chance of sustaining that change. Over the coming chapters, I want to give you more tools to further equip you with all the skills you need to keep it going for the rest of your life.

We all have habits that we want to give up or change for something a little healthier. It could be something big or small but something you have always wanted to change. Well, now is the time to make that a priority, put that habit at the forefront of your goals and use all of the endorphins that you will be creating with exercise to help you stay focused and break that habit. This is where this book is different to anything else you have tried. As you begin to feel better, have more energy and change your outlook on life, all of a sudden that habit will no longer be foremost in your mind – you will realise that it wasn't that important to you in the first place. As you become more confident in your own skin, you will realise that you *can* do it, that you *won't* fail this time and that you *will* do it.

Here are some common habits I have seen clients change and some tips to help you on your journey to breaking them.

SMOKING

Smoking is seriously addictive and has links to so many illnesses. Once seen as cool, it is now known as being damaging to your health. It can be one of the tougher habits to break and you need to replace the habit of smoking with something else. Guess what? The 30-day plan is perfect for helping you to break this cycle. You replace the dreaded cigarette with exercise and nutrition, giving you a great focus that will get you through the worst of it. This will also help you combat the classic post-cessation weight gain, which is caused by boredom more than anything else.

Two simple but important things to have in your diet when you are giving up smoking, and even if you aren't, are apples and apple cider vinegar. These help to break up the tar in the lungs and also phlegm. Ideally take three small spoonfuls of apple cider vinegar in boiling water – this improves the effect and you can add a little more if you like acidic flavours, as I do.

SUGAR

Sugar is one of the main causes of the obesity epidemic of the past 50 years. We have drastically increased our intake, as it is hidden in many foods under lots of different names to confuse you. Basically any ingredient with 'ose' at the end of it tends to be sugar, for example fructose and sucrose. Even many products that are supposedly healthy are actually laden with sugar, mostly the fat-free and low-fat products. There are many issues with sugar, from the health consequences to its energy effects. The biggest issue from my perspective is the weight problem. Sugar triggers fat storage – once your glycogen levels (the muscles' fuel) are full, the rest will store as fat. It is also seriously addictive so you end up craving more and more. Now, I am not suggesting you give up sugar for life, as that's far too strict to last. But limit it to a treat day or two and enjoy it for what it is. When giving up sugar you can expect headaches or spots and even fatigue. The good news is that this goes away after the first few days and with plenty of water in your day you will get through it.

COFFEE OR TEA

These have become staples of the modern diet. Caffeine stimulates you when tired, makes you alert and focused and can be addictive too. It also tends to come with snacks, adding plenty of calories to your day that you really don't need. Like sugar, caffeine is addictive. It isn't great for your body and can be a hard habit to break. I always say that one or two a day will do you no harm at all. But if you are one of those people who have five or more a day, you need to put this top of your list of habits to break. The withdrawal symptoms can be similar to reducing sugar intake – headaches, fatigue, mood swings and poor skin – but, again, with plenty of water you will find these pass. Ride the storm of the first few days and watch just what a difference it can make to your life.

GRAZING

Grazing is generally what people do who don't structure their food intake during the day. You pick at foods, big and small, and never really feel full. You often don't realise you are doing it and gain weight but can't figure out how. Firstly you need to keep a food diary and see just what you are eating during the day. Once you can see it written down it will make a big difference – and then it's time to tackle this habit! By following the 30-day method, eating three meals a day and two snacks, you will feel fuller, healthier and will also lose weight.

NEGATIVITY

Negativity is something that will bring you down, stop you from achieving your goals and generally cause you more harm than good. When you are trying to achieve something, some people will knowingly or unknowingly try to stop you from doing it. One of my own rules is to cut negative people from my life. People who try to hold me back are not helping me to achieve my goals, so I simply move on. I have cut friends and others from my life for this reason and have never had any regrets. I am a driven person with goals, and through hard work and plenty of luck I have achieved these goals. This means that I have missed nights out, birthdays and holidays and other events due to work. My good friends know me and know that it's nothing personal and I value their support. By eliminating negativity from your life you will feel free, motivated, happy and have a zest for life. Life is too short to be spent being held back by others, so take a look where negativity is in your life and see what you can do to change it. I firmly believe that it's important to surround yourself with positive people and that this will help you to achieve your goals. Positive people will also make you feel good, motivated and eager to work towards what you are striving for.

The reality is that no matter what your habit is, the lessons that you have learnt in the past 30 days will help you to break anything. Decide upon what habit you are going to kick, set the goal of keeping to the food and exercise plan that you have learnt for the 30 days and let me help you achieve something you never thought possible: a new way of living.

The whole idea of the Slim Solution is to use exercise and nutrition and my guidance over the course of the plan to help you live in a new way. By adding regular exercise into your day and by eating better, you will wake up in the morning with a zest for life, with goals set to work towards and realising how great it feels to be healthy, energised and ready to take on life. So put all your fears to one side, park those excuses that you used before, jump in feet first and break that habit: follow what I am asking you to do and you will wonder why you haven't felt like this before, why you couldn't do it before and just what was stopping you.

5

WELLBEING – THE NEW YOU

FULFIL

YOUR

POTENTIAL

Breaking bad habits, exercising more and eating better are all working towards one thing: wellbeing! Wellbeing is one of the buzz words of the past year and in my opinion it is one of the greatest benefits of getting healthy and getting fit. While it can be great to lose weight and fit into your clothes better, health and wellbeing are the serious benefits that will last for the rest of your life.

But what is wellbeing and how is it measured? There are various definitions but I think that it is a combination of six different elements:

- **Life evaluation:** on a scale of one to ten, how a person feels about their general life. How do you rate yours?

- **Aerobic health:** how healthy are you? Use the resting heart-rate test later in the book to test your aerobic health.

- **Physical health:** use the tests later in the book to look at your physical health.

- **Emotional health:** how much people experience happiness, stress, anger and even depression.

- **Healthy behaviour:** how often people exercise and eat healthily.

- **Work environment:** how much support people receive at work and how they feel they are treated.

This book is designed to help you get the most out of life. It will turn you on to exercise and health. It will help you directly with five of the above elements. Through making the right changes to your diet and getting your body moving over the last 30 days you are already halfway there.

Wellbeing is very much a way of living, an approach to life and a way of thinking. I have spent many years perfecting the Slim Solution plan with my clients and the fact that it is sustainable is something that, I feel, stands out and separates me from my competitors. I meet clients one and two years later and am always delighted to see that they have kept up their hard work and the results they achieved during the sessions have stayed with them.

Real wellbeing is accomplished through a combination of the three elements that you have seen in this book:

- Motivation

- Nutrition

- Exercise

The reality is that all of these are co-dependent: one won't work without the other. All the exercise in the world won't be effective if you are eating take-aways every night. By changing your diet alone you won't get the lean muscle tissue or tone that you are looking for and that will make the big difference to how you look in your clothes. Without motivation and goal setting nothing can really happen either. These are also the cornerstones of breaking those habits that you could never break before.

WHAT DIFFERENCES CAN WELLBEING MAKE?

- **Energy:** Your body will be functioning properly and you will be bounding with energy and focus. You will get more done during the day and have plenty leftover for everything else in life.

- **Better sleep:** You will sleep deeper and better than before as your stress levels reduce and your mind is clearer going to bed. Deep sleep is the body's re-energiser and is the best way to recharge your body and rest your muscles.

- **Lower cholesterol:** Cholesterol is extremely controversial at the moment, with two very different schools of thought. One says that the food we eat directly affects our cholesterol levels and the other says that it doesn't. Regardless, we know that exercise can certainly help lower it and by improving your diet you can make a big difference to your cholesterol. I have seen this so often with my clients, resulting in reductions in medication and often eliminating medication altogether.

- **Lower blood pressure:** As with cholesterol levels, the Solution can help to lower your blood pressure. It could also help to eliminate medication. Follow the 30 days and get your bloods rechecked with your GP – watch what a difference such a short space of time can make.

- **Slimmer waistline:** While wellbeing is about being healthy, one of the benefits is reducing your waistline. Don't forget your waist is not at your hips where your jeans sit: it's around your bellybutton. The lower the measurement here, the lower your risk of cardiovascular disease and the healthier you are. Less than 40 inches for men and 37 inches for women would be rough guidelines to aim for.

- **Lighter weight:** On your journey to wellbeing, your waistline will come down and so will your weight. As your body rejuvenates itself, becoming healthy again, you will begin to lose weight slowly and safely. Remember, each pound of fat you are trying to lose equals 3,500 calories. And, no, muscle is not heavier than fat, although muscle is certainly denser and takes up less space.

- **Sense of fulfilment:** One of my favourite benefits of this programme is the sense of fulfilment that comes with it. Your outlook on life becomes more positive, your clothes feel better and you feel healthier. You look in the mirror one day and think to yourself, I look good, I feel good and life is good!

- **Happiness:** The happier you are with yourself, the happier you become with life and everything that comes with it. You change from a pessimist to an optimist, so you deal with all life throws at you much more easily, no longer reacting negatively like you once did.

All of these elements combined will improve your wellbeing. By coming through the 30 days of the plan you will have made many of these changes already, and by continuing with those changes you will have made wellbeing part of your life.

TIPS FOR SUCCESS

1. Do what you love – find a workout that works for you. There are endless routines and methods out there, but if you find one that you enjoy this will ensure you stick at it and get the results.

2. Make your goal visible. Take a picture or cut out an image that you associate with your goal and place it in your diary, on the fridge or anywhere where you know you will see it on a regular basis.

3. Remember to trust in the process – patience is key when starting a new fitness programme or exercise routine. It will take time before the results start showing, so keep the faith. Patience and persistence equal success!

4. Drinking five cups of green tea each day has been shown to raise your metabolism and it is rich in antioxidants. Try it with a slice of fresh lemon to help the body detox.

5. When eating out, ask the waiter to take away the bread at the start of your meal and always order a side salad when the option is available. Have salad

dressings on the side and if you're concerned about large portion sizes order two starters instead of a starter and a main meal.

6. Oily fish is high in essential omega-3 fats and includes salmon, mackerel, trout, herring, fresh tuna and sardines. Fish is also a great source of protein and contains many vitamins and minerals so aim to eat at least two portions a week.

7. Leave calorie-filled 'junk food' at the grocery store. If you only buy fresh foods, you will only eat fresh foods. Stock your cupboard with nutritious options only and you will

not be tempted to go for that chocolate bar.

8. Whatever small change you make today, remember that you are one step closer than yesterday. Gradual changes over time amount to great things.

9. Though it may be the last thing you feel like doing when you're tired, exercise, even a brisk walk, can be more effective than a nap or cup of coffee at fighting fatigue.

10. Choose fresh, seasonal and local produce from your butcher or grocer. This will ensure you are getting the best-quality food available while supporting local businesses.

6

MEASURE YOUR FITNESS

READY

CHANGE

ACHIEVE

Now that we have looked at habits and how to change them, and we have looked at the basis of wellbeing and its positive effects, I want to take a look at fitness and give you some simple tools to measure your own fitness levels.

Fitness can mean different things to people, so I think it is important to be able to identify what 'fit' means to you. There are many different types of fitness, so I will introduce you to the most common types. Let's take a look and see which ones you need to work on.

AEROBIC

This is the one that applies to everyday life. Aerobic fitness is the ability of the lungs and heart to supply oxygen to the body where required. Put simply, it is the fitness you use to walk to the shops, go up the stairs, run, swim and so on. If you find that any of these activities causes you to get out of breath very quickly, you need to work on this! The better your aerobic fitness, the better your lifestyle health will be. We know there is a direct link between aerobic fitness and health and living longer.

To measure your aerobic fitness, take your resting heart rate in the morning before you get out of bed. To do this, simply place your right index and middle fingers to the right side of your neck, just under your jawline. You should feel a pulse. Now count the number of beats for 15 seconds and multiply by four. This will give you a number – the lower the number, the fitter you are. Here is a rough guide:

- **Lower than 50:** you are very fit, with a good aerobic base

- **Between 50 and 60:** you are pretty fit and above average

- **Between 60 and 70:** you are reasonably fit and in the normal category for the population

- **Between 70 and 80:** you certainly need to improve your aerobic fitness but with some work you will see it improve quite quickly

- **Between 80 and 90:** you are unfit and it is likely to affect your lifestyle – when you start exercising it should be very gradual. Don't push yourself too hard

- **Between 90 and 100:** you are very unfit and should seek GP clearance before starting any exercise programme

- **Over 100:** go to your GP and get a full checkup

Once you have taken your resting heart rate, make a note of it and track it once a week to see what impact your training is having on your heart. This plan is designed to lower your resting heart rate by using cardiovascular exercise and resistance exercise. The lower the number, the more efficient your heart is becoming – the heart is a muscle and can grow stronger. But remember to take your resting heart rate just once a week – ideally on the same day, as you get a more reliable marker.

The reason for taking it in the morning before you get out of bed is because you haven't taken any stimulants that could speed up your heart rate, such as coffee or tea.

STRENGTH

The next type of fitness I am going to talk to you about is strength. Now don't get scared – I'm not talking about how much weight you can lift or push or pull. Strength, in my eyes, is more about how capable your body is in dealing with everyday life. Sure, there is another side of strength which is all about how much you can squat, but I'm not interested in that, nor are my clients and I'm guessing that you aren't either. The reality is that the stronger the muscles in your body are, the firmer and more toned they will be. You will be able to stand longer, walk further and lift things without getting pain like before. You will be able to carry bags from the shop without having to stop and rest your arms. This is what I deem strength to be. All of the exercises in this book are about improving your strength but without using weights. Simple body-resistance exercises will deliver all the results you could ever need. You will have firm, toned arms, legs and bum, which will no longer wobble when you move or look in the mirror. You will feel more confident in your clothes and, even more importantly, out of them! But my favourite benefit is that life becomes better: you feel better and stronger and can do more. Your metabolism, which is your inbuilt rev counter and controls the rate at which you burn calories, will be higher as a result of doing resistance exercises.

If you are reading this and have arthritis or osteoporosis, then you above all people need to do resistance exercises. The stronger the muscles around the joint, the more support they can give you and help alleviate your pain. So many people stop exercising when they get these conditions, yet weight-bearing exercise is one of the best ways to help improve them!

FLEXIBILITY

Flexibility is a type of fitness that most people forget about, especially men! Yet it is pretty crucial for your body, especially as you begin to get older. A supple body is a healthy body, with fewer injuries and joint problems. If lower back pain is a problem for you then flexibility is something you especially need to look at, as you more than likely have tight hamstrings that are pulling on your back and causing the pain. The beauty of flexibility fitness is that, unlike strength and aerobic fitness, the classes and workouts that will help are far more chilled out and relaxed. As you get older, you may prefer these styles and they can be especially good for dealing with stress too. Classes like yoga, Pilates, body balance and tai chi can all help to improve your flexibility.

A quick way to test your flexibility fitness is to sit on the ground, feet out in front, toes pointed towards you. Take a pen or pencil in your hand and now sit up tall, posture straight. Gently bring your hands forward and try to touch your toes. Use the pen or pencil to mark where you get to on the floor. Come back every week and try again to see how you are progressing.

HEALTH

The Slim Solution is primarily about health. No

matter what your goal is, health is one of the reasons you want to start a plan like this. The healthier the body, the longer you live, the better you feel and the more you will enjoy life. Health is a type of fitness that combines the three we have already looked at. No matter what your goal may be, I think that health is the underlying goal for us all. Combine aerobic fitness, strength and flexibility and you will be fit in all three ways, but you will also be healthy: really healthy. Your body is such an amazing machine that it will adapt quickly to training. You will become healthy, with a lower resting heart rate, smaller waistline, more muscle tone and more flexibility than before. Health is what I want this book to deliver for you. Lifelong health. The changes you have made over the past 30 days will have already shown you just how it feels to be healthy.

7

KITCHEN AND COOKING
ESSENTIALS

GRILL

COLOUR

COOK

I CAN'T COOK

I am not a great cook myself but I have some simple tips that I think will make all the difference to your kitchen and how you prepare your food. Many of us find it hard to make time to cook and rely on processed foods for all our meals. One of the big changes you will have made over the past 30 days will have been to eat less processed foods and prepare foods a little more.

The reality is that food can be cooked just as quickly from fresh with the right utensils. Food and nutrition are a key part of any plan and the Slim Solution is no different. If weight loss is your goal, you can't just use exercise to achieve it. Food counts for at least 60 per cent initially in terms of losing weight and getting healthy: it really is that important.

For the past 30 days we have used food as a natural cleanser and detox aid – to increase your fibre and fluid intakes to flush the body of built-up waste. I also use nutrition to give you back your energy and zest for life, increasing the amount of vitamins, minerals and antioxidants you eat.

You will also notice that there are no supplements on the plan, as I believe you should obtain your nutrients from real food as opposed to taking tablets or shakes. This book also contains super healthy and easy-to-make recipes that will show you just how simple it is to prepare healthy food. If I can make it then anyone can!

WHAT EVERY KITCHEN SHOULD HAVE

- **Wok:** A wok will cook pretty much anything with very little oil on a lower heat than a frying pan. The result is fresher, crunchier, healthier vegetables and meat that is really tender. Great for stir-fries and even cooking meat on its own.

- **George Foreman grill:** One of the classics that no kitchen should have to do without. It is basically a double-sided grill which cooks food quickly and safely. I have cooked most things on this when in a rush and it is probably the easiest way to cook anything.

- **Steamer:** While I must admit I don't get to eat as much steamed food as I would like, it is a fantastic way to cook and keep as many nutrients packed into the food as possible. It leaves your vegetables soft and nutritious. You can either buy an electric steamer or inserts for your existing saucepans, which are just as easy to use.

- **Griddle pan:** This is one of my recent discoveries and I find it a great way to cook meats with serious flavour, giving a barbecue-style taste. Again it makes food easy to cook without using much oil, and it means that you are grilling food as opposed to frying it, which is always good.

- **Nuts and seeds jar:** I find this a fantastic idea for snacks. Find a good-sized glass jar and empty your favourite nuts and seeds into it, give it a good shake and you can then use the mix in stir-fries, on your porridge, as a snack and also on natural yoghurt. Remember a handful of nuts is good for you – although high in calories, they are the right type of calories and the right type of fats.

- **Spices and seasonings**: I love flavours and spices and can think of nothing better to have in your kitchen than different spices ready to use. Don't forget that spicy food is incredibly good for you and your metabolism, helping to lower your fat levels, so add as much as you want!

- **Colour**: A nutritionist friend of mine always recommends colour as the most important thing to have on your plate at meal times. The more colours you have, the more antioxidants and enzymes that are in the food, and they are super good for you. So don't be afraid to mix it up and try as many new colourful foods as possible.

- **No microwave:** Needless to say, I am not a microwave fan. I believe that it isn't good for the stomach, the body or the skin. Microwaved food continues to cook while you are digesting it, as the molecules heat so quickly then keep on heating for approximately 30 minutes while you are eating. You will find that most foods that you microwave can be cooked quickly and healthily in other ways.

TIPS FOR SUCCESS

1. Be productive with your workout time – estimate how long your session will take and ensure that you finish in that amount of time or less. Once you begin to create deadlines, your

workout becomes more efficient and the results increase dramatically.

2. Start your day with a glass of water, as your body loses water while you sleep, leaving you naturally dehydrated in the morning. A glass of water when you get up will wake the senses and help start your day fresh.

3. Eating small, healthy snacks throughout the day will help keep your stomach full and stop you from running to the vending machine at around 4 pm. Not just any snack will do, however – avoid processed, pre-packaged foods, as

these are high in sugar and preservatives.

4. Switch to whole grains – over time, eating whole grains (brown rice, whole wheat bread, wholegrain pasta) in place of refined grains (white rice, white bread, white pasta) makes it easier to control weight and lowers the risk of both heart disease and diabetes.

5. Simplify things – instead of counting calories and measuring food portions, think of your diet in terms of colour, variety and freshness. As you experiment with recipes, your diet will become healthier and more delicious.

6. Make small changes – nothing changes overnight, so take small steps at the beginning and build it up week by week. You may start to feel the benefits within the first two weeks, but it can be much later before you begin to see them.

7. Fly with the eagles if you want to be an eagle yourself – eliminate people and situations which no longer make you happy or have a purpose in your life. People change and so do you.

8. Keeping a food diary will teach you more than any book. This is a great way to review your food habits

and to make small changes to your daily intake. Try keeping one for a full week to see exactly where there is room for improvement.

9. Focus on the type of fat rather than the amount of fat in your diet. Good fats are essential to physical and emotional health and come from foods like fish, avocados, olives and walnuts.

10. When grocery shopping, work your way around the outer perimeter of the store – this is usually where the fresh, unrefined produce can be found, with all the sugar-rich, artificial foods stocked in the centre aisles.

8

THE FOOD BACKGROUND

REAL

NUTRITIOUS

HEALTHY

Food is crucial to health and to weight loss. In this chapter I will explain my philosophy on food and why it's beneficial to eat the way I recommend in the plan.

GI

I believe the glycaemic index is very important – that's why I am recommending it in the 30-day plan. I use it, my clients use it and I have seen the benefits again and again. What's more, I know that its effects last long term – it simply becomes a way of eating and a lifestyle choice. It's easy to follow and will make such a difference to your life.

This low-GI style of eating will:

• improve your energy levels

- improve your skin, hair and nails

- help you lose weight

- help lower your blood pressure, your cholesterol and your diabetes risk

- improve how you deal with stress and work pressure

- decrease the side effects of menstruation

These are just some of the benefits of eating a low-GI diet. There are many others. I have eaten this way for years and all of my clients eat this way too.

SO WHAT IS GI ALL ABOUT?

GI is simply the reaction of the sugar in your blood to the food that you eat. Some foods cause a high reaction in blood sugar, some a low reaction. Foods that are high-GI cause a big increase in blood sugar, triggering a greater insulin response from your liver, which promotes fat storage in your body once your glycogen stores (fuel tanks to the muscles) are full. High-GI foods also cause a surge of energy that can be followed by a hypoglycaemic reaction (low blood sugar) two to three hours later. This explains why your body craves more high-sugar foods soon after you have eaten them, creating the sugar cycle that causes you to gain weight. High GI foods tend to be high in refined sugar, which has no health benefits at all, merely giving you energy rushes and promoting fat storage within your body. On the other hand, low-GI foods give a slow increase in energy over a longer time. Your body uses more of the energy from these foods and stores less as fat. You will feel fuller for longer, have less cravings and have more energy.

Now that you know what GI is all about, you have the power to learn what foods will deliver what type of energy and also what foods will promote weight loss/weight gain. Here is a quick swap list with some of the more common foods:

HIGH GI	LOW GI
White bread	Brown bread
White rice	Brown rice
White pasta	Brown pasta
Most processed cereals	All-Bran
Fizzy drinks	Water
Flavoured water	Water with diced fruit
Potatoes	Sweet potatoes
Cream-based sauces	Tomato-based sauces

These are just a few examples to show you that by making simple choices you can change the GI content of the food you are eating – it really is that easy. If you want to do some further research, just google 'GI lists' and you will see pretty much every food's GI number listed. A GI of under 50 is considered low, but the problem with this is that food labels don't have GI numbers on them. More products and supermarkets are beginning to put low-GI labels on certain foods but not nearly enough so, as opposed to giving you GI lists of products, I am going to give you an even easier tool to check the healthy status of a food product before you buy it. You are essentially looking for one key ingredient on a food label. This one nutrient will tell you if the product is going to add to that waistline or help you to reduce it. That nutrient is sugar.

Sugar has become the enemy of waistlines all around the world. Fat as a nutrient is no longer the be-all and end-all – we now know that fat can have positive health effects in the body. But sugar is in all high-GI foods, and when it enters your bloodstream it will send your energy levels through the roof, triggering insulin production in your body, promoting fat storage.

Sugar will also have effects on your skin, increasing the dryness and the occurrence of spots. From now on, I want you to look at the sugar content in the foods that you are eating. Look at the food label on the back of the packet: under carbohydrates you will see an 'of which sugars' value. The lower this value, the better the food. Ideally, aim to have a sugar content of less than 50 per cent of the carbohydrate value.

Products that have 'sugar free' and 'diet' on the front generally contain an additive called aspartame. It is sweeter than sugar, cheaper than sugar and has pretty much the same effect as sugar. The worst part, for your waistline, is that it also causes your body to produce insulin, just like sugar does. Insulin forces your body to promote fat. So although it may say 'diet' on the cover, actually it is causing the same reaction in your body that sugar would. So you can definitely add aspartame to your list of foods to avoid.

Low GI has nothing to do with counting calories – life is for living, not counting calories. I just feel that you should eat until you are full, enjoy your food and lose weight. Yes I said it: no calorie counting, enjoying your food and losing weight too. It can be done!

TREAT MEALS AND WHY THEY ARE IMPORTANT

I am sure that you were surprised to see that I allowed you a treat meal each week on the plan. The whole idea of my plan is that it becomes something that you do for the rest of your life. In terms of food, one of the key ways in which it becomes a lifelong habit is by having one day a week to eat your favourite dish that we all know isn't good for you, which I believe in moderation will do you no harm at all. If you love chocolate, don't have it every day but maybe have it after your treat meal as a dessert and have the best that you can buy. Treats should be the best quality possible. Remember, you are trying to break habits for life and get healthy for life, so why should you try to cut everything out? You shouldn't!

FLUID AND DRINKS

ALCOHOL

Every other quick fix on the market will insist

that you give up all alcohol for the course of their plan. As this isn't a quick fix, the good news is that you won't have to give it up at all. Whatever drink you enjoy, your treat day is your time to have it. Different drinks have ingredients that can affect your body in different ways. Let's take a look at some of the common ones and what they do:

- **Beer:** Beer is probably my least favourite, as it tends to be full of yeast. Yeast will bloat the stomach and can even ferment, causing more bloating.

- **Cider:** Cider is high in sugar, which gives it its sweetness. Ideally go for the organic ones that haven't been as processed, as they are certainly somewhat better for you.

- **Wine:** Yes, red wine has more antioxidants but this doesn't necessarily mean it's healthier for you and wine is certainly high in sugar. Champagne is my recommendation here, as it tends to be of a higher quality and people tend to drink less of it – although there is yeast in the champagne.

- **Spirits and mixers:** These are generally the best option. Go for the normal mixers as opposed to the diet versions as they are better.

Obviously there is more to fluid than just alcohol! Let's look at some other drinks.

WATER

Your body needs water and lots of it. All of the major bodily functions require water, yet so many people spend the day dehydrated, which affects pretty much everything, from weight loss to energy to productivity. More often than not, the feeling of hunger is actually a dehydration sign, not a signal that your body needs food. By drinking fluids regularly during the day, you will be keeping your body functioning properly and helping it to eliminate toxins and fat by going to the toilet on a regular basis. If you haven't drunk water regularly for quite some time, one of the instant effects will be visiting the toilet a lot, which is a great sign, as it's your body regulating itself, excreting the excess fluid and toxins that it was holding onto. This will settle down after a week or so to a more regular pattern.

So how much water should you be drinking? Two litres is the normal recommendation, unless you are being seriously active – then you may need to increase it. The easiest way of ensuring that you are drinking the right amount is to fill a two-litre bottle of water every morning and aim to have the bottle empty by the end of the day. Flavoured water should be avoided, as this has a lot of sugar in it, but if you find still water too plain then chop up some pieces of fruit, such as a lemon or an orange, and put this into the water to flavour it naturally.

SOFT DRINKS

A can of fizzy drink can contain as much as 12 spoons of sugar and does little or nothing for your hydration levels, as the sugar is just giving you energy and promoting fat storage. As in the rest of this plan, balance is the whole idea and a soft drink every now and again won't do you any harm, just not on a regular basis.

JUICES

Juices are best avoided unless they are freshly squeezed, as most of the juices on supermarket shelves are pasteurised to within an inch of their nutritional lives and provide serious amounts of sugar per glass. Fruit juice in its natural form only lasts about two to three days in the fridge, yet the juice on supermarket shelves lasts for months – in my view, meaning much of the goodness is lost.

SMOOTHIES

Smoothies don't count towards your fluid intake either, I am afraid. These have become very popular over the past few years and are actually very high in calories, especially the off-the-shelf versions. Try to make them at home for the healthiest option, like my smoothie recipe later in the book.

NOT ANOTHER QUICK FIX

From a nutritional perspective, I suppose the real message I want to give you is that this plan isn't just another quick fix. I am not telling you to quit carbohydrates, eat extremely high levels of protein or lots of fat. I am saying that you should be eating everything in moderation and having one day a week where you can have what you want. The whole concept of the plan is that over the 30 days I show you just how easy eating healthily can be and that exercise isn't as scary as you thought it might be. The other aim of this book, and both of my other books, is to educate you as much as possible, as I believe the more you know about food and exercise, the easier it is to make healthy choices. Knowledge is power when it comes to exercise and nutrition and with this book you will be learning as well as getting results.

9

THE SLIM SOLUTION RECIPES

SUCCEED

BELIEVE

WORK HARD

BREAKFAST

BAKED EGGS WITH TABASCO AND TOMATO SALSA

1 tomato, chopped in 1cm dice

A few drops of Tabasco

1 spring onion, chopped finely

A little fresh coriander, chopped

2 eggs

A drizzle of olive oil

Use the olive oil to grease a small ramekin. Heat the oven to 180 degrees and break the two eggs into the greased ramekin. Place in the oven for 15 minutes approximately, until just set. Meanwhile mix the chopped tomato, spring onion and coriander with some Tabasco and place on top of the eggs when they come out of the oven.

GRILLED TOMATO, SAUTÉED SPINACH AND BROWN TOAST

1 slice of wholegrain bread, toasted
1 teaspoon of olive oil
½ supermarket bag of baby spinach (100g approx.)
1 large tomato, cut in half

Heat the grill, place the cut tomato on a tray under it and cook for 8–10 minutes. Meanwhile heat the olive oil in a frying pan and cook the baby spinach until it is wilted. Place the spinach on the slice of brown toast and place the tomato on top.

POACHED EGGS ON BROWN TOAST

1 slice of wholegrain bread, toasted
2 eggs
1 tomato, grilled (optional)

Heat a small saucepan of water until it comes to a boil. Turn the heat down to low and break two eggs into the water. Cook for three–four minutes until eggs are cooked to your liking and drain them by lifting them out with a slotted spoon. Place on a slice of brown toast and serve with the grilled tomato, if using.

MUSHROOMS ON BROWN TOAST

1 slice of wholegrain bread, toasted
1 teaspoon of olive oil
Large handful of mushrooms of your choice, sliced

Heat the olive oil in a frying pan. When hot add the handful of mushrooms and season with plenty of black pepper. Cook for five–six minutes on a high heat until the mushrooms are cooked through and then serve on the slice of brown toast.

BERRIES WITH LOW-FAT YOGHURT AND TOASTED OATS

A handful of fresh berries, such as blueberries and strawberries, washed
2 tablespoons of porridge oats
2 tablespoons of low-fat yoghurt

Heat a dry frying pan and place the oats in the pan. Toast for five–seven minutes on a medium heat until they are golden brown. Allow to cool then mix with the prepared berries and the yoghurt.

BOILED EGGS WITH ASPARAGUS SOLDIERS

2 eggs
6–8 spears of asparagus

Bring a small saucepan of water to the boil. Using a spoon, slide in the eggs and then pop in the asparagus. Set a timer for four minutes (for a perfect soft yolk and set white). Drain and serve the asparagus on the side to dip.

HUEVOS RANCHEROS

Brown wrap
2 tablespoons of tinned black beans or kidney beans
1 egg
Tomato salsa:
1 tomato, chopped in 1cm dice
1 spring onion, finely chopped
A little fresh coriander, chopped
Dash of Tabasco

First make the salsa – just mix the chopped ingredients with some Tabasco to taste. Poach one egg using the instructions above for Poached eggs on brown toast. Meanwhile heat the beans in a small saucepan (a little Tabasco in these is good too). Finally heat the wrap in a frying pan. To assemble, place the wrap on a plate, cover with the hot beans, next the salsa and finally the drained poached egg.

GINGERED PEAR SMOOTHIE

100ml of low-fat milk
1 ripe pear
1 small apple
1 teaspoon of honey
Pinch of ground ginger
2 tablespoons of raw porridge

Blend the fruit, milk, porridge, honey and ginger in a liquidiser or smoothie maker until thoroughly mixed. Serve immediately.

SMOKED SALMON AND BROWN BAGEL

1 brown bagel, toasted
100g approx. of smoked salmon
Squeeze of lemon juice

Serve the salmon on top of the bagel and squeeze lemon juice over.

LUNCH

DELICIOUS SOUP TO KEEP YOU GOING ALL DAY!

1 tablespoon of olive oil
1 onion, chopped
1 clove of garlic, chopped
1 courgette, chopped
2 peppers, chopped
2 tins of chopped tomatoes
1 litre of chicken or vegetable stock
2 carrots, chopped
Handful of broccoli florets

Handful of green beans
Handful of shredded cabbage or spinach
4 sticks of celery
Few drops of Tabasco or 1–2 whole chillies, chopped

Fry the onion in the olive oil for 3–4 minutes until softened. Add the garlic and the remaining vegetables, which should be in even-sized chunks. Cook for a few minutes, then add the tinned tomatoes and the stock, and the chilli or Tabasco if using. Cook for 15 minutes approximately until the vegetables are tender. You can either purée the soup or leave it chunky.

SEAFOOD SALAD

50g approx. of ready-to-eat mixed seafood such as prawns, white crab meat, fresh salmon or smoked salmon
2 large handfuls of rocket or mixed lettuce
10 cherry tomatoes, halved
A small cucumber, sliced

Few slices of red onion
½ red pepper, sliced
½ tablespoon of lemon juice
½ tablespoon of olive oil

Mix the lemon juice and the olive oil for the dressing with some black pepper. Assemble the salad on a plate and drizzle the dressing over everything including the fish.

COS LETTUCE SALAD WITH ORANGES, GREEN BEANS AND FLAKED ALMONDS

2 handfuls of washed, chopped cos lettuce
1 handful of green beans
1 handful of broccoli florets
1 orange, peeled with a knife and sliced into rings
1 tablespoon of toasted flaked almonds
½ tablespoon of lemon juice
½ tablespoon of olive oil

Bring a small pan of water to the boil and cook the green beans for five–six minutes.

Refresh under cold water. Meanwhile mix the cos, raw broccoli florets, orange rings, cooled green beans and flaked almonds together. Mix the lemon juice and olive oil and use this to dress the salad.

CHICKEN AND SPINACH SALAD WITH BABY PEAS AND MINT

100–150g of baby spinach
1 cold cooked chicken breast, sliced in strips
2 tablespoons of cold, cooked frozen peas
1 teaspoon mint, chopped
5 cherry tomatoes, halved
A few slices of cucumber
½ tablespoon of balsamic vinegar
½ tablespoon of olive oil

Mix the olive oil and balsamic vinegar to make the dressing. Then mix together the ingredients for the salad. Dress at the last minute to keep fresh.

BAKED SWEET POTATO WITH ROAST VEGETABLES

1 sweet potato
1 pepper, chopped
1 courgette, chopped
½ aubergine, chopped
1 teaspoon of olive oil
Pinch of rosemary or thyme leaves, dried or fresh

Pierce the sweet potato several times with a fork and bake in the oven at 180 degrees for an hour or until tender. For the final 20 minutes, place the chopped vegetables onto a roasting tray with the olive oil and rosemary or thyme in the same oven and cook until tender. Split the sweet potato in half and top with the roasted vegetables.

TUNA SALAD WITH HARD-BOILED EGG

Small tin of tuna in brine or spring water
1 egg

Small handful of green beans
6 cherry tomatoes, halved
Large handful of rocket leaves
A little sliced red onion
10 olives
Squeeze of lemon juice

Cook the green beans and the egg in the same small saucepan of water – the beans for about five minutes, the egg for eight. Then put both in a colander under cold running water to cool. Peel and chop the egg. Assemble the salad by mixing everything together and dress with the lemon juice.

MOROCCAN CHICKPEA AND CARROT SALAD

1 small tin of chickpeas
½ teaspoon of ground cumin
Juice of ½ lemon
1 tablespoon of olive oil
2 carrots, chopped thinly

Handful of coriander or mint, chopped
1 small head of baby gem lettuce, sliced
1 tablespoon of toasted flaked almonds
A little crushed garlic (optional)
A dash of Tabasco (optional)

Mix the chickpeas with the carrots, the chopped coriander or mint, the flaked almonds and the gem lettuce. Mix the cumin, lemon juice and olive oil – and garlic and Tabasco if using. Dress the salad with this mixture and serve immediately.

LOW-FAT HUMMUS WITH TOASTED PITTA AND SALAD

1 small tin of chickpeas
Juice of ½ lemon
2 tablespoons of tahini paste
½ teaspoon of ground cumin
1 clove of garlic

Purée the drained chickpeas with the lemon juice, cumin, tahini, garlic and a little water to loosen the mix. Serve with toasted brown pitta, halved cherry tomatoes, pepper and cucumber batons and some black olives.

DINNER

TURKEY ESCALOPE WITH TOMATO SALSA AND GREEN SALAD

150g of turkey escalope
Juice of ½ lemon
1 teaspoon of olive oil
1 tomato, chopped in 1cm dice
A few drops of Tabasco
1 spring onion, chopped finely
A little fresh coriander, chopped

Marinate the turkey in the olive oil and lemon juice for a few minutes. Meanwhile prepare the salsa by mixing the chopped tomato, spring onion and coriander with some Tabasco. Heat a grill or a griddle pan and cook the turkey: this will take five minutes approximately, depending on thickness. Serve the turkey with the salsa on top and a green mixed-leaf salad on the side.

GRILLED STEAK WITH CHERRY TOMATO AND MIXED LEAVES

150–175g lean steak of your choice, grilled to your liking
Huge handful of mixed leaves
10 cherry tomatoes, halved
A few small florets of raw broccoli
A squeeze of lemon juice
A teaspoon of olive oil

Mix the salad ingredients together and dress with the lemon juice and olive oil while you cook the steak.

CHICKEN BREAST WITH RATATOUILLE

1 red onion, chopped
1 clove of garlic, chopped
1 punnet of cherry tomatoes, halved
1 courgette, chopped
1 aubergine, chopped
1 yellow pepper, chopped
10–12 basil leaves, chopped
2 teaspoons of olive oil
1 chicken breast

Fry the onion and garlic in one teaspoon of the olive oil. When soft, turn the heat off. Meanwhile place the vegetables, apart from the cherry tomatoes, on a roasting tray with the other teaspoon of olive oil and roast for twenty minutes at 180 degrees until tender. Add the halved cherry tomatoes for the final ten minutes of cooking time. Add the vegetables to the onion and garlic and mix well. Meanwhile, grill or bake the chicken breast until cooked through and serve with the ratatouille.

BROWN PASTA WITH QUICK TOMATO AND OLIVE SAUCE

1 small onion, chopped

1 teaspoon of olive oil

1 clove of garlic

A few drops of Tabasco

4 tomatoes, chopped

1 red pepper, chopped

10 black olives, sliced

10 basil leaves, chopped

Cook some brown pasta. While this is cooking heat the olive oil in a saucepan. Add the onion and crushed garlic and cook for three–four minutes. Add the chopped tomatoes, the chopped pepper and the Tabasco and cook for a further five minutes. Add the basil and olives. Drain the pasta and mix everything together.

BAKED SALMON WITH FENNEL

1 salmon fillet
½ bulb of fennel, thinly sliced
Juice of ½ lemon
Pepper
Thyme leaves, dried or fresh

Take a large sheet of tin foil and fold it in two. Place the thinly sliced fennel onto one side of the tin foil and place the salmon on top. Squeeze the lemon juice over the fish and season with pepper and thyme. Fold over the foil and seal it to keep everything secure. Cook in a preheated oven at 180 degrees for approximately 15 minutes. Beware when opening the foil as it can get steamy! Serve with some green salad.

BAKED SEA BASS WITH STIR-FRIED VEGETABLES

1 teaspoon of sunflower oil
1 clove of garlic, crushed

2 scallions, chopped

A little grated ginger

1 red pepper, sliced

1 pak choi, chopped

A handful of tender-stem broccoli

A handful of sugar snap peas

150g sea bass fillet

1 teaspoon of soy sauce

1 tablespoon of coriander, chopped

Heat the oven to 180 degrees and place the sea bass on a baking tray lined with parchment paper. Cook for 8–10 minutes, depending on thickness. Meanwhile heat the sunflower oil in a wok. Add the scallions, garlic and ginger and cook for a minute. Add the pepper, broccoli and sugar snaps and cook for two minutes. Add the pak choi, coriander and soy sauce and cook for a further minute. Serve with the sea bass.

GRILLED CHICKEN AND STEAMED GREEN VEGETABLES

1 chicken fillet
Small handful of sugar snap peas
Small handful of broad beans, shelled
Small handful of broccoli
Small handful of green beans
Small handful of asparagus stems, cut in half
1 teaspoon of olive oil
Squeeze of lime juice

Grill or bake the chicken fillet until cooked through. Meanwhile, get your steamer ready and add the vegetables. The green beans and broccoli will take the longest so add these first; after a minute or two add the asparagus and broad beans; and finally add the sugar snaps after another minute and cook for three minutes. Dress the vegetables in the lime juice and olive oil and serve with the chicken.

THAI CHICKEN AND BROWN NOODLE BROTH

1.5 pints of chicken broth or stock
1 small bunch brown noodles (generally, the packets are two servings so check and break in half if this is the case)
1 chicken breast, cut in long thin strips
1 small handful of sugar snap peas, cut in half lengthways
½ chilli, chopped
Juice of ½ a lime
1 teaspoon of soy sauce
A few drops of fish sauce
1 tablespoon of coriander, chopped

Heat the stock in a saucepan and add the noodles and chicken at the same time. Cook for three–four minutes until both are cooked through. Add the sugar snaps, chilli, lime juice, soy and fish sauce. Cook for a further minute. Add the fresh coriander and serve.

HALIBUT WITH ROCKET SALAD AND GRILLED COURGETTE

150–175g piece of halibut or similar white fish
1 medium-sized courgette, sliced lengthways
1 teaspoon of olive oil
Handful of rocket leaves
Squeeze of lemon juice

Heat a griddle pan until smoking. Pour the teaspoon of olive oil over the halibut and courgette and rub in. Place both on the griddle pan and cook on each side for three minutes approximately, depending on thickness. The trick is to use a high heat and not to move the food about too much. The fish and courgette should both take similar times to cook. When cooked, serve the halibut with a salad made from rocket leaves and the warm courgette dressed in a little lemon juice.

BABA GANOUSH

1 brown pitta
3 large aubergines
2 cloves of garlic
1 lemon, juiced
3 teaspoons of tahini paste
4 tablespoons of olive oil

Pierce the skins of the aubergines and place into a 150-degree oven until the skin is black (this gives it a smoky flavour). Take out of the oven and scrape the flesh from the skins. Add to a blender with the other ingredients, except the pitta, and blend. Alternatively, put all the ingredients into a bowl and whisk until they form a paste. Serve with the brown pitta or vegetables.

JAPANESE MARINATED BEEF WITH CUCUMBER PICKLE

150–175g steak of your liking
1 tablespoon of teriyaki sauce
½ cucumber

2 teaspoons of lime juice
1 teaspoon of sesame oil
Few drops of Tabasco
Small head of baby gem lettuce

Marinate the steak in the teriyaki sauce for 10 minutes or so. Slice the cucumber thinly and squeeze the lime juice over it. Add the sesame oil and Tabasco and leave to marinate for 10 minutes. Meanwhile cook the steak on the grill, griddle pan or barbecue. Allow to rest for a few minutes then slice thinly. Slice the baby gem lettuce and mix with the cucumber pickle, the steak and any juices.

KARL'S SUPERFOOD VEGETABLE SOUP

426g tin of white beans, rinsed and drained
2 medium to large carrots, sliced
3 medium broccoli florets
1 large onion, diced
1 red pepper, sliced

1 yellow pepper, sliced
2 cloves garlic, minced or sliced thinly
2 medium sweet potatoes, diced
½ teaspoon of dried basil
½ teaspoon of dried oregano
1 or 2 bay leaves
1 tablespoon of soy sauce
Freshly ground black pepper to taste
2 organic vegetable stock cubes

Put all the ingredients into a pot and add enough water to cover. Cook until the vegetables are soft. Blend and serve immediately and don't forget to freeze the leftovers.

HEALTHY SNACKS

- 2 tablespoons of low-fat hummus (see recipes for lunch) and a sliced red pepper

- Ryvita spread with a teaspoon of no-sugar peanut butter

- A Granny Smith apple or a mandarin orange

- 50g of turkey breast or grilled chicken breast

- A small pot of low-fat Greek yoghurt with a half teaspoon of honey

- 10 olives, any kind

- Small mixed salad made from rocket, cherry tomatoes, sugar snap peas, cucumber and balsamic vinegar

- 2 celery sticks and a handful of sugar snap peas

- A pear and ten whole almonds

- A Ryvita spread with a teaspoon of hummus and sliced cucumber

TIPS FOR SUCCESS

1. Kick up the intensity – a lot of people focus on the length of their workout rather than the effort they put in. Half an hour at full intensity can be just as effective as a one-hour workout at a moderate pace – make every minute count to maximise results.

2. Remember to drink water throughout the day. Water speeds up our metabolism, helping our bodies to burn fat while we work. Its health benefits are well documented so take regular breaks from your desk to visit the water dispenser.

3. Vegetables should ideally be steamed as much as possible. Most of the nutrients are lost in the water when you boil vegetables, so use a steamer whenever you can. When the weather is good, throwing them on the barbecue is also a better choice.

4. Don't skip breakfast. Breakfast really is the most important meal of the day – it gets the metabolism burning after a night of fasting and gives you the energy you need to take on the day. Try some organic oats with skimmed milk and berries for that slow-release energy you need.

5. Have a treat – people often think of healthy eating as an all-or-nothing proposition, but in fact the key to maintaining a balanced diet is moderation. Allow yourself a treat meal once a week.

6. Keep your eyes on the prize – having a goal in place will keep you motivated on your journey. From getting in shape for a party to running your first 5K, knowing where you're headed will keep you moving in the right direction.

7. Prep your meals at the beginning of the week. Take a couple of hours to plan your meals, do a grocery

shop, chop your veggies, boil your eggs and freeze meals that can be easily re-heated if you get in late from work.

8. Remember that it is not our problems that cause us stress, it's avoiding them. Often once we get started the task is not as bad as we anticipated, and sometimes getting started is the hardest part – break it down into smaller tasks and this will eliminate a lot of stress.

9. Get a minimum of seven hours' sleep every night. Insufficient sleep sends the body's hormones into a state of chaos, causing

mindless snacking and mood swings throughout the day. Your body needs to rest and re-set to function properly, so give it the sleep it needs.

10. Don't think diet, think nutrition. The word diet automatically brings about negative thoughts and associations. Stop reading about the latest fad diet and start thinking nutrient-rich foods – and lots of them!